Study Guide

for use with

SOCIOLOGY
A Brief Introduction

Fifth Edition

Richard T. Schaefer
DePaul University

Prepared by
Richard T. Schaefer
DePaul University
and
Cheryl Tieman
Radford University

Mc Graw Hill

Boston Burr Ridge, IL Dubuque, IA Madison, WI New York San Francisco St. Louis
Bangkok Bogotá Caracas Kuala Lumpur Lisbon London Madrid Mexico City
Milan Montreal New Delhi Santiago Seoul Singapore Sydney Taipei Toronto

The McGraw·Hill Companies

Mc Graw Hill

Study Guide for use with
SOCIOLOGY: A BRIEF INTRODUCTION
Richard T. Schaefer

Published by McGraw-Hill, an imprint of The McGraw-Hill Companies, Inc., 1221 Avenue of the Americas, New York, NY 10020.

2 3 4 5 6 7 8 9 0 CUS/CUS 0 9 8 7 6 5 4 3

ISBN 0-07-282417-4

www.mhhe.com

CONTENTS

INTRODUCTION

This study guide is designed to enhance your understanding of the discipline of sociology and to help you prepare for examinations covering *Sociology: A Brief Introduction*, 5th Edition, by Richard T. Schaefer. Careful use of this supplement will assist you in reviewing discussions of sociological theory, important research findings, and social policy sections.

The study guide has been developed specifically to provide you with a clearer understanding of the assigned material. The organization is identical to that of the textbook: each chapter in the study guide corresponds directly to one of the 16 chapters in *Sociology: A Brief Introduction*, 5th Edition. Within each chapter of the study guide, the material is presented in the same sequence as in the textbook and is keyed to page numbers in the text. Consequently, if you have problems with a particular subject or study guide exercise, you can return to the relevant pages in the text for further study.

You may find some sections of the study guide more helpful than others, but you should probably use all sections for the first few chapters until you learn what works best for you. Regardless of which sections you utilize, the study guide will be most valuable if you have read the textbook first. The purpose of the study guide is to assist you in reviewing the material after you have read an entire chapter of the text. We recommend waiting a day *after* reading the chapter and then turning to the study guide.

A *chapter outline* begins each chapter of the study guide; it presents the major topics of the chapter in the same order in which they appear in the text. If you review this outline and immediately recognize certain areas in which your comprehension is weak, you should probably return to the text before continuing your work with the study guide.

After the chapter outline comes a section of *key points*. In this section, 10 to 14 short excerpts from the chapter are summarized in paragraph form, with glossary items highlighted and page references provided. These key points summarize the most important themes and concepts discussed in the chapter; they should be studied carefully before you proceed to later exercises in the study guide.

A list of *key terms* is included in each chapter of the study guide; each glossary item is presented in the order in which it appears in the textbook. Space is provided so that you can test yourself by filling in the definition of each term. Although these key terms appear in boldface in the text, this section of the study guide offers another opportunity to reinforce your understanding of the basic concepts used by sociologists. You may be tempted to check them off as you think to yourself, "I remember that," but it is important to write out the answers in the study guide. The very act of writing them out will reinforce your mastery of these terms. Once you have finished, you can check your answers against the correct definitions, which are included in the same study guide chapter.

The *self-test* for each chapter allows you to examine understanding of the text material. Each self-test includes 15 *modified true-false questions*, 15 *multiple-choice questions*, and 15 *fill-in questions*. Page references and correct answers are provided for all sections of the self-test. Students will often ask, "Are the practice questions similar to the 'real' test questions?" The publisher materials for this course have been created in an integrated team approach. Therefore, if your instructor is using test material that is part of this package, there should be a high level of consistency between your Study Guide questions and the questions that you see on your tests.

To gain the greatest benefits from the self-test sections, do not use them after a hurried initial skimming of the chapter. Instead, use the self-test as a practice examination only after you have thoroughly studied the textbook material. As you take the test, note your weak areas; keep track of the questions on which you find yourself guessing. Recognize how you may be misreading or misinterpreting certain types of questions. After you check your answers, return to and reread the textbook passages where your comprehension was weak. Even if your instructor uses broad short-answer questions or essay questions on examinations, you will find the exercises in the self-test helpful in improving your understanding of the material in the textbook.

For each of the chapters in the textbook that ends with a social policy section, there is a corresponding exercise on *understanding social policy* in the study guide. These exercises ask questions about the social policy material in the text. Space is provided for your responses, and correct answers are included later in the study guide chapter.

In addition to this study guide, the Reel Society Interactive Movie CD-ROM included with your textbook and the Online Learning Center (the text's companion website) are valuable tools to help you study and master the material in the textbook. The CD-ROM features an interactive movie that demonstrates the sociological imagination through the use of actors and scenarios involving campus life. The program allows you to interact with the concepts described in the textbook in a relevant and meaningful context. A wide variety of issues and perspectives are addressed in order to relate major sociological concepts and theories to your everyday life. The Online Learning Center, located at www.mhhe.com/schaefer5, offers interactive quizzes and maps, social policy exercises, Census 2000 updates, chapter glossaries, vocabulary flashcards, and additional resources.

Effective use of the Reel Society Interactive Movie CD-ROM, the Online Learning Center Website and this study guide, along with effective study habits, will ensure that your introduction to the discipline of sociology will be both meaningful and enjoyable.

Cheryl Tieman
Radford University

CHAPTER 1

UNDERSTANDING SOCIOLOGY

KEY POINTS

Sociology as a Field of Study: **Sociology** is the systematic study of social behavior and human groups. It focuses primarily on the influence of social relationships on people's attitudes and behavior, and on how societies are established and change. (3)

The Sociological Imagination: In attempting to understand social behavior, sociologists rely on an unusual type of creative thinking. C. Wright Mills described such thinking as the **sociological imagination**—an awareness of the relationship between an individual and the wider society. A key element in the sociological imagination is the ability to view one's own society as an outsider would, rather than from the limited perspective of one's personal experiences and cultural biases. (3)

Sociology as a Science: The term **science** refers to the body of knowledge obtained by methods based upon systematic observation. Just like other scientific disciplines, sociology engages in organized, systematic study of phenomena (in this case, human behavior) in order to enhance understanding. In contrast to other social sciences, sociology emphasizes the influence that society has on people's attitudes and behavior and examines the ways in which people shape society. (6)

Sociological Theory: Within sociology, a **theory** is a set of statements that seeks to explain problems, actions, or behavior. An effective theory may have both explanatory and predictive power. That is, it can help us develop a broad and integrated view of the relationship between seemingly isolated phenomena, and to understand how one type of change in an environment leads to others. An essential task in building a sociological theory is to examine the relationship among bits of data gathered through research, which may seem completely unrelated. (8)

Early Thinkers—Comte, Martineau, and Spencer: Auguste Comte coined the term sociology to apply to the science of human behavior. He believed that a theoretical science of society and a systematic investigation of behavior were needed to improve society. Harriet Martineau (1820–1876) offered insightful observations of the customs and social practices of both her native Britain and the United States. Herbert Spencer (1820–1903) adapted Charles Darwin's evolutionary view of the "survival of the fittest" by arguing that it is "natural" that some people are rich while others are poor. (9)

Émile Durkheim: Émile Durkheim was appointed as one of the first professors of sociology in France. Above all, Durkheim will be remembered for his insistence that behavior must be understood within a larger social context, not just in individualistic terms. Durkheim concluded that, like other forms of group behavior, religion reinforces a group's solidarity. Another of Durkheim's main interests was the consequences of work in modern societies. (10)

Max Weber: Max Weber (1864–1920), a German sociologist, told his students that they should employ ***Verstehen***, the German word for "understanding" or "insight," in their intellectual work. To fully comprehend behavior, we must learn the subjective meanings people attach to their actions—how they themselves view and explain their behavior. We also owe credit to Weber for the key conceptual tool of the **ideal type**. In his own works, Weber identified various characteristics of bureaucracy as an ideal type. (10)

Karl Marx: Under the analysis of Karl Marx (1818–1883), society was fundamentally divided between classes who clash in pursuit of their own class interests. When Marx examined the industrial societies of his time, he saw the factory as the center of conflict between the exploiters (the owners of the means of production), and the exploited (the workers). In *The Communist Manifesto*, which first appeared in 1848, Marx and Friedrich Engels (1820–1895) argued that factory workers (whom they referred to as **proletariat**) should unite to fight for the overthrow of capitalist societies. (11)

Charles Horton Cooley: Charles Horton Cooley (1864–1929) preferred to use the sociological perspective to look first at smaller units—intimate, face-to-face groups, such as families, gangs, and friendship networks. He saw these groups as the seedbeds of society in the sense that they shape people's ideals, beliefs, values, and social nature. Cooley's work increased our understanding of groups of relatively small size. (12)

Functionalist Perspective: In the view of functionalists, society is like a living organism in which each part of the organism contributes to its survival. Therefore, the **functionalist perspective** emphasizes the way that parts of a society are structured to maintain its stability. For over four decades, Harvard University sociologist Talcott Parsons (1902–1979) dominated sociology in the United States with his advocacy of functionalism. Parsons saw any society as a vast network of connected parts, each of which contributes to the maintenance of the system as a whole. (13)

Conflict Perspective: In contrast to functionalists' emphasis on stability and consensus, conflict sociologists see the social world in continual struggle. The **conflict perspective** assumes that social behavior is best understood in terms of conflict or tension between competing groups. Expanding on Marx's work, conflict theorists are interested in how society's institutions, including the family, government, religion, education, and the media may help to maintain the privileges of some groups and keep others in a subservient position. One important contribution of conflict theory is that it has encouraged sociologists to view society through the eyes of those segments of the population who rarely influence decision making, such as Blacks and women. (14)

Conflict Perspective—A Racial View: One important contribution of conflict theory is that it has encouraged sociologists to view society through the eyes of those segments of the population that rarely influence decision-making. Early Black sociologists, such as W.E.B. Du Bois (1868–1963), conducted research that they hoped would assist the struggle for a racially egalitarian society. (15)

Interactionist Perspective: The **interactionist perspective** generalizes about fundamental or everyday forms of social interaction in order to understand society as a whole. It is a sociological framework for viewing human beings as living in a world of meaningful objects. The "objects" may include material things, actions, other people, relationships, and even symbols. George Herbert Mead (1863–1931) is widely regarded as the founder of the interactionist perspective. (15)

Feminist Perspective: The **feminist perspective** views inequity in gender as central to all behavior and organization. Because it clearly focuses on one aspect of inequality, it is often allied with the conflict perspective. But unlike conflict theorists, those who hold to the feminist perspective often focus on the micro-level relationships of everyday life, just as interactionists would. Drawing on the work of Marx and Engels, contemporary feminist theorists often view women's subordination as inherent in capitalist societies. (16)

KEY TERMS

Briefly define or identify the following terms in the spaces provided below. The definitions of these terms can be found later in this chapter of the study guide.

Sociology	Anomie
Sociological imagination	*Verstehen*
Science	Ideal type
Natural science	Macrosociology
Social science	Microsociology
Theory	Functionalist perspective

Manifest functions	Nonverbal communication
Latent functions	Dramaturgical approach
Dysfunction	Feminist perspective
Conflict perspective	Social Inequality
Interactionist perspective	

SELF-TEST

MODIFIED TRUE-FALSE QUESTIONS: If the statement below is true, write "true" in the space provided. If the statement is false, briefly correct the error.

1. Sociology is concerned only with how major social institutions like the government, religion, and the economy affect us.

2. In the aftermath of natural disasters, a community's social organization and structure tend to collapse.

3. Émile Durkheim concluded that the suicide rates of a society reflected the extent to which people were or were not integrated into the group life of the society.

4. French theorist Émile Durkheim coined the term *sociology*.

5. The French sociologist Harriet Martineau applied Charles Darwin's evolutionary concepts to societies.

6. When Max Weber discussed the ideal bureaucracy, he was focusing on the best type of organization that was possible.

7. Karl Marx argued that the working class needed to overthrow the existing class system.

8. Émile Durkheim was the first modern-day sociologist to focus on small groups and relationships.

9. George Herbert Mead emphasized that sociology should strive to bring together the "macro" and "micro" level approaches to the study of society.

10. Microsociology concentrates on large-scale phenomena or entire civilizations.

11. Talcott Parsons dominated sociology in the United States for over four decades with his advocacy of the interactionist perspective.

12. Throughout most of the twentieth century, sociology in the United States was influenced primarily by the conflict perspective.

13. George Herbert Mead is widely regarded as the founder of the interactionist perspective.

14. Interactionists see symbols as an especially important part of human communication.

15. Ida Wells-Barnett used her analysis of society as a means of resisting oppression. In her case, she researched what it meant to be African American, a woman in the United States, and a black woman in the United States.

MULTIPLE-CHOICE QUESTIONS: In each of the following, select the phrase that best completes the statement.

1. Sociology is concerned with
   a. social behavior and human groups.
   b. the behavior of an individual.
   c. random human actions.
   d. all of the above

2. Which of the following is most closely associated with the concept of the sociological imagination?
   a. Émile Durkheim
   b. Max Weber
   c. Karl Marx
   d. C. Wright Mills

3. In his study of suicide, Émile Durkheim was primarily concerned with
   a. suicide rates and how they varied from country to country.
   b. personalities of individual suicide victims.
   c. means people used to take their own lives.
   d. effects of suicide on the families of victims.

4. In *Society in America*, which early sociologist gave special attention to status distinctions and to such factors as gender and race?
   a. Émile Durkheim
   b. Max Weber
   c. Auguste Comte
   d. Harriet Martineau

5. Which one of the following concepts did Max Weber introduce to the field of sociology?
   a. dramaturgy
   b. ideal types
   c. functionalism
   d. macrosociology

6. *The Communist Manifesto* was written by
   a. Karl Marx and Georg Hegel.
   b. George Herbert Mead and Jane Addams.
   c. Friedrich Engels and Karl Marx.
   d. Talcott Parsons and Robert Merton.

7. Which sociologist co-founded the famous Chicago settlement house called Hull House?
   a. Charles Horton Cooley
   b. Jane Addams
   c. George Herbert Mead
   d. C. Wright Mills

8. Robert Merton's contributions to sociology include
   a. successfully combining theory and research.
   b. an analysis of deviant behavior that focuses on societal goals and means.
   c. an attempt to bring macro and micro level analyses together.
   d. all of the above

9. Which sociological perspective views society as a network of connected parts, each of which contributes to the maintenance of the system as a whole?
   a. the functionalist perspective
   b. the conflict perspective
   c. the interactionist perspective
   d. the dramaturgical perspective

10. A university that serves as a meeting ground for people seeking marital partners is performing
   a. a manifest function.
   b. a latent function.
   c. a dysfunction.
   d. a manifest dysfunction.

11. Karl Marx's view of the struggle between social classes inspired the contemporary
   a. functionalist perspective.
   b. conflict perspective.
   c. interactionist perspective.
   d. dramaturgical approach.

12. Which of the following was an early Black sociologist, active in the struggle for a racially egalitarian society, who was critical of theorists who seemed content with the status quo?
   a. Harriet Martineau
   b. Herbert Spencer
   c. Booker T. Washington
   d. W.E.B. Du Bois

13. Perhaps the major theme of analysis in sociology today is ______________—a condition in which members of society have differing amounts of wealth, prestige, or power.
   a. macrosociology
   b. the dramaturgical approach
   c. *Verstehen*
   d. social inequality

14. Which sociological perspective examines sports on the micro level by focusing on how day-to-day social behavior is shaped by the distinctive norms, values, and demands of the world of sports?
    a. the functionalist perspective
    b. the conflict perspective
    c. the interactionist perspective
    d. the psychological perspective

15. Sports perpetuate the false idea that success can be achieved simply through hard work, while failure should be blamed on the individual alone (rather than on injustices in the larger social system). This statement would most accurately represent which perspective?
    a. the functionalist perspective
    b. the conflict perspective
    c. the interactionist perspective
    d. the feminist perspective

FILL-IN QUESTIONS: Fill in the blank spaces in the sentences below with the correct words. Where two or more words are required, there will be a corresponding number of blank spaces.

1. Sociology focuses primarily on the influence of ______________ ______________ on people's attitudes and behavior and on how societies are established and change.

2. While the findings of sociologists may at times seem like common sense, they have been ______________ by researchers.

3. ______________ ______________ noted that while suicide is a solitary act, it is related to group life, and that Protestants, unmarried individuals, and soldiers were more likely to commit suicide than Catholics, married individuals, and civilians.

4. In *Society in America*, originally published in 1837, English scholar ______________ ______________ examined religion, politics, child rearing and immigration in the young nation.

5. ______________ ______________ adapted Charles Darwin's evolutionary view of the "survival of the fittest" by arguing that it is "natural" that some people are rich while others are poor.

6. ______________ ______________ concern for a value-free, objective sociology was a direct response to Marx's deeply held convictions.

7. _____________ _____________ pioneering work has led contemporary sociologists to focus on how membership in a particular gender classification, age group, racial group, or economic class affects a person's attitudes and behavior.

8. In the early 1900s, sociologist _____________ _____________ saw smaller groups as the seedbeds of society.

9. Émile Durkheim's cross-cultural study of suicide, examinations of international crime rates, stereotypes of Asian Americans as a "model minority," and population patterns of Islamic countries are all examples of _____________.

10. _____________ _____________ saw society as a vast network of connected parts, each of which helps to maintain the system as a whole.

11. The university's role in certifying academic competence and excellence is an example of a _____________ function.

12. In contrast to functionalists' emphasis on stability and consensus, _____________ theorists see the social world in continuous struggle.

13. _____________ scholars have argued for a gender-balanced study of society in which women's experiences and contributions are as visible as those of men.

14. _____________ theory is built on conflict theory in that it sees gender differences as a reflection of the subjugation of women by men.

15. The _____________ perspective would note that participation in sports may promote friendship networks that permeate everyday life.

DEFINITIONS OF KEY TERMS

Sociology: The systematic study of social behavior and human groups. (3)

Sociological imagination: An awareness of the relationship between an individual and the wider society. (3)

Science: The body of knowledge obtained by methods based upon systematic observation. (6)

Natural science: The study of the physical features of nature and the ways in which they interact and change. (6)

Social Science: The study of various aspects of human society. (6)

Theory: In sociology, a theory is a set of statements that seeks to explain problems, actions, or behavior. (8)

Anomie: The loss of direction felt in a society when social control of individual behavior has become ineffective. (10)

Verstehen: The German word for "understanding" or "insight" used by Max Weber to stress the need for sociologists to take into account people's emotions, thoughts, beliefs, and attitudes. (10)

Ideal type: A construct or model that serves as a measuring rod against which actual cases can be evaluated. (11)

Macrosociology: Sociological investigation that concentrates on large-scale phenomena or entire civilizations. (13)

Microsociology: Sociological investigation that stresses study of small groups, and often uses laboratory experimental studies. (13)

Functionalist perspective: A sociological approach that emphasizes the way that parts of a society are structured to maintain its stability. (13)

Manifest functions: Open, stated, and conscious functions. (14)

Latent functions: Unconscious or unintended functions; hidden purposes. (14)

Dysfunction: An element or a process of society that may disrupt a social system, or lead to a decrease in stability. (14)

Conflict perspective: A sociological approach that assumes that social behavior is best understood in terms of conflict or tension between competing groups. (14)

Interactionist perspective: A sociological approach that generalizes about fundamental or everyday forms of social interaction. (15)

Nonverbal communication: The sending of messages through the use of posture, facial expressions, and gestures. (16)

Dramaturgical approach: A view of social interaction, popularized by Erving Goffman, under which people are examined as if they were theatrical performers. (16)

Feminist perspective: A sociological approach that views inequity in gender as central to all behavior and organization. (16)

Social inequality: a condition in which members of society have differing amounts of wealth, prestige, or power. (18)

ANSWERS TO SELF-TEST

Modified True-False Questions

1. Sociology is a broad field of study that examines social institutions, and how others influence behavior. (3)
2. In the aftermath of natural disasters, greater social organization and structure emerge to deal with a community's problems. (7)
3. True (8)
4. The term *sociology* was coined by Auguste Comte. (9)
5. Herbert Spencer applied Charles Darwin's evolutionary concepts to societies. (10)
6. When Max Weber discussed the ideal bureaucracy, he was providing a useful standard for measuring how bureaucratic an actual organization was. (11)
7. True (12)
8. Charles Horton Cooley was the first modern-day sociologist to focus on small groups and relationships. (12)
9. Robert Merton emphasized that sociology should strive to bring together the "macro" and "micro" level approaches to the study of society. (13)
10. Macrosociology concentrates on large-scale phenomena or entire civilizations. Microsociology stresses study of small groups. (13)
11. Talcott Parsons dominated sociology in the United States for over four decades with his advocacy of the functionalist perspective. (14)
12. Throughout most of the twentieth century, sociology in the United States was influenced primarily by the functionalist perspective. (14)
13. True (16)
14. True (16)
15. True (16)

Multiple-Choice Questions

1. a (3)
2. d (3)
3. a (8)
4. d (9)
5. b (11)
6. c (11)
7. b (12)
8. d (13)
9. a (14)
10. b (14)
11. b (15)
12. d (15)
13. d (18)
14. c (19)
15. b (19)

Fill-In Questions

1. social relationships (3)
2. tested (7)
3. Émile Durkheim (8)
4. Harriet Martineau (10)
5. Herbert Spencer (10)
6. Max Weber's (11)
7. Karl Marx's (12)
8. Charles (Horton) Cooley (12)
9. macrosociology (13)
10. Talcott Parsons (14)
11. manifest (14)
12. conflict (14)
13. Feminist (16)
14. Feminist (16)
15. interactionist (19)

CHAPTER 2 SOCIOLOGICAL RESEARCH

KEY POINTS

The Scientific Method: The scientific method is a systematic, organized series of steps that ensures maximum objectivity and consistency in researching a problem. There are five basic steps in the scientific method: defining the problem, reviewing the literature, formulating the hypothesis, selecting the research design, and then collecting and analyzing data and developing the conclusion. (28)

Defining the Problem: The first step in any research project is to state as clearly as possible what you hope to investigate. An operational definition is an explanation of an abstract concept that is specific enough to allow a researcher to measure the concept. (29)

Formulating the Hypothesis: After reviewing earlier research and drawing on the contributions of sociological theorists, the researchers formulate the hypothesis: a speculative statement about the relationship between two or more factors known as variables. A **variable** is a measurable trait or characteristic that is subject to change under different conditions. If one variable is hypothesized to cause or influence another one, social scientists call the first variable the **independent variable**. The second is termed the **dependent variable** because it is believed to be influenced by the independent variable. (30)

Collecting and Analyzing Data: In most studies, social scientists must carefully select what is known as a sample. A representative sample is a selection from a larger population that is statistically typical of that population. The most frequently used representative sample is a random sample in which every member of the entire population has the same chance of being selected. (30)

Validity and Reliability: The scientific method requires that research results be both valid and reliable. **Validity** refers to the degree to which a measure or scale truly reflects the phenomenon under study. **Reliability** refers to the extent to which a measure provides consistent results. (32)

Surveys: A **survey** is a study, generally in the form of an interview or questionnaire, which provides sociologists with information concerning how people think and act. Among the United States' best-known surveys of opinion are the Gallup poll and the Harris poll. Surveys can be indispensable sources of information, but only if the sampling is done properly and the questions are worded correctly. (33)

Observation: Investigators who collect information through direct participation and/or observation of a group, tribe, or community under study are engaged in observation. This method allows sociologists to examine certain behaviors and communities that could not be investigated through other research techniques. In some cases, the sociologist actually "joins" a group for a period of time to gain an accurate sense of how it operates. This is called **participant observation**. (35)

Experiments: When sociologists want to study a possible cause-and-effect relationship, they may conduct **experiments**. An experiment is an artificially created situation that allows the researcher to manipulate variables. In the classic experimental method, two groups of people are selected and matched for similar characteristics such as age or education. The **experimental group** is exposed to an independent variable; the **control group** is not. (36)

Use of Existing Sources: Sociologists do not necessarily have to collect new data in order to conduct research and test hypotheses. The term **secondary analysis** refers to a variety of research techniques that make use of publicly accessible information and data. Many social scientists find it useful to study cultural, economic, and political documents including newspapers, periodicals, radio and television, tapes, scripts, diaries, songs, folklore, and legal papers, to name a few examples. In examining these sources, researchers employ a technique known as **content analysis**, which is the systematic coding and objective recording of data, guided by some rationale. (37)

Ethics of Research: The American Sociological Association (ASA), the professional society of the discipline, first published the **Code of Ethics** in 1971. It includes the following basic principles: maintain objectivity and integrity in research, respect the subject's right to privacy and dignity, protect subjects from personal harm, preserve confidentiality, seek informed consent from research participants, acknowledge research collaboration and assistance, and disclose all sources of financial support. (39)

Neutrality and Politics in Research: Max Weber believed that sociologists must practice **value neutrality** in their research. In his view, researchers cannot allow their personal feelings to influence the interpretation of data. Investigators have an obligation to accept research findings even when the data run contrary to their own personal views, to theoretically based explanations, or to widely accepted beliefs. The issue of value neutrality does not mean you can't have opinions, but it does mean you must work to overcome any biases, however unintentional, that you may bring to the research. (40)

Technology and Sociological Research: The increased speed and capacity of computers has enabled sociologists to handle much larger sets of data. Anyone with a desktop computer and a modem can access information to learn more about social behavior. The Internet is an inexpensive way to reach large numbers of potential respondents, and to get a quick return of responses. However, the ease of access to information has led to new research problems: How do you protect a respondent's anonymity, and how do you define the potential audience? (41)

Studying Human Sexuality: The controversy surrounding research on human sexual behavior raises the issue of value neutrality. This becomes especially delicate when one considers the relationship of sociology to the government, particularly when one fears that findings critical of government institutions will jeopardize chances of obtaining federal support for future research projects. In 1991, the U.S. Senate, led by Senator Jesse Helms and other conservatives voted 66–34 to forbid funding any survey on adult sexual practices. Nevertheless, the researchers raised $1.6 million of private funding to make their study possible. Social scientists argue that using data from research helps us more wisely address such public policy issues as AIDS, sexual harassment, rape, welfare reform, sex discrimination, abortion, teenage pregnancy, and family planning. (43)

KEY TERMS

Briefly define or identify the following terms in the spaces provided below. The definitions of these terms can be found later in this chapter of the study guide.

Scientific method	Random sample
Operational definition	Validity
Hypothesis	Reliability
Variable	Control variable
Independent variable	Research design
Dependent variable	Survey
Causal logic	Interview
Correlation	Questionnaire

Representative sample	Observation
Qualitative research	Hawthorne effect
Ethnography	Secondary analysis
Quantitative research	Content analysis
Experiment	Code of ethics
Experimental group	Value neutrality
Control group	

SELF-TEST

MODIFIED TRUE-FALSE QUESTIONS: If the statement below is true, write "true" in the space provided. If the statement is false, briefly correct the error.

1. The second step in the scientific method is formulating the hypothesis.

2. The dependent variable in a hypothesis is thought to cause or influence the independent variable.

3. Television viewers and radio listeners who email their views on today's headlines or on political contests are participating in a random sample.

4. After collecting and analyzing data, the researchers come to the final step in the scientific method: creating a theory.

5. Sociologists classify the Gallup poll and the Harris poll as examples of observation research.

6. There are two main types of samples: the interview and the questionnaire.

7. In *Street Corner Society*, William F. Whyte revealed his identity to the men he was studying and joined in their conversations, bowled with them, and participated in other leisure-time activities.

8. The control group is exposed to an independent variable; the experimental group is not.

9. Worker productivity in the Hawthorne studies diminished when researchers observed them because the employees became self-conscious.

10. The most frequently used existing sources in sociological research are census data, crime statistics, newspapers, and periodicals.

11. The American Sociological Association's (ASA) Code of Ethics requires sociologists to maintain objectivity, preserve confidentiality, report all illegal behavior to appropriate authorities, and acknowledge research collaboration and assistance.

12. In William Zellner's 1978 study of fatal car accidents or "autocide" he followed the basic principals in the ASA's Code of Ethics.

13. On the basis of his research concerning automobile accidents, sociologist William Zellner concluded that at least 12 percent of all fatal, single-occupant crashes are suicides.

14. Rick Scarce, a doctoral candidate in sociology, agreed to testify before a grand jury in 1993 and share with them research findings on his study of environmental protestors.

15. Émile Durkheim's assertion that suicide was the result of social forces rather than supernatural forces was an illustration of a sociologist maintaining value neutrality.

MULTIPLE-CHOICE QUESTIONS: In each of the following, select the phrase that best completes the statement.

1. The first step in any sociological research project is to
   a. collect data.
   b. define the problem.
   c. review previous research.
   d. formulate a hypothesis.

2. Formulating the hypothesis is the ______________ step in the scientific method.
   a. first
   b. second
   c. third
   d. fourth

3. In most instances, how well a student does on a test is determined by how much the student studies for it. In this example, studying for an exam is a
   a. correlation.
   b. independent variable.
   c. dependent variable.
   d. sample.

4. When selecting a random sample, a researcher
   a. administers a questionnaire to every fifth woman who enters a business office.
   b. examines the attitudes of residents of a city by interviewing every twentieth name in the city's telephone book.
   c. studies the attitudes of Democratic voters by choosing every tenth name found on a city's list of registered Democrats.
   d. all of the above

5. A detailed plan or method for obtaining data scientifically is called a(n)
   a. sample.
   b. experiment.
   c. research design.
   d. scientific method.

6. In order to genuinely reflect a broad range of the population, a survey must be based on precise
   a. representative sampling.
   b. experiments.
   c. surveys.
   d. hypotheses.

7. A researcher can obtain a higher response rate by using which type of survey?
   a. interviews
   b. questionnaires
   c. representative samples
   d. observation techniques

8. The study of interracial friendships conducted by Tom Smith, head of the General Social Survey, was an example of
   a. observation research.
   b. a survey.
   c. content analysis.
   d. an experiment

9. William F. Whyte's study of a low-income Italian neighborhood in Boston was a classic example of
   a. participant-observation research.
   b. a survey.
   c. content analysis.
   d. an experiment.

10. Which one of the following is exposed to an independent variable?
   a. the control group
   b. the representative group
   c. the experimental group
   d. none of the above

11. An instructor wants to determine if giving essay tests increases student learning. In one class that the instructor teaches, she continues to test as she has always done. In another class, she gives the students essay questions. She then measures the differences in learning, if any, between the two classes. The class that is given essay questions is the
   a. control group.
   b. representative group.
   c. experimental group.
   d. correlation group.

12. A researcher examines the literature written by Black novelists during the "Negro Renaissance" (1913–1935) to see if they reflect the political movements going on in the Black community in the United States at that time. What type of research methodology is being used in this example?
    a. secondary analysis
    b. interviews
    c. observation
    d. content analysis

13. Which one of the following statements is not part of the Code of Ethics developed by the American Sociological Association?
    a. Acknowledge research collaboration and assistance.
    b. Preserve the confidentiality.
    c. Protect subjects from personal harm.
    d. Make all research notes available for public scrutiny.

14. Max Weber
    a. recognized that it is impossible for scholars to prevent their personal values from influencing the questions that they select for research.
    b. stressed that researchers had to maintain the confidentiality of their subjects.
    c. emphasized that under no conditions could a researcher allow his or her personal feelings to influence the interpretation of data.
    d. both a and c

15. Which one of the following is a finding of the National Health and Social Life Survey?
    a. Well-educated and affluent women are more likely to have abortions than are poor teens.
    b. Adults in the United States have sex 2-3 times per week.
    c. Forty-seven percent of all women reported that they had been coerced into a sexual encounter at some time.
    d. Eleven percent of men and nine percent of women stated that they were homosexual or bisexual.

FILL-IN QUESTIONS: Fill in the blank spaces in the sentences below with the correct words. Where two or more words are required, there will be a corresponding number of blank spaces.

1. Unlike the typical citizen, the sociologist has a commitment to the use of the _____________ method in studying society.

2. The scientific method includes the following steps: defining the problem, reviewing the _____________, formulating the hypothesis, selecting the research design, and collecting and analyzing data, and developing the conclusion.

3. In formulating a _____________, researchers generally must suggest how one aspect of human behavior influences or affects another.

4. A hypothesis is a speculative statement about the relationship between two or more factors known as _____________.

5. In the hypothesis, the more an individual eats the more the individual weighs, how much a person eats is a (an) _____________ variable.

6. In order to test a hypothesis and determine if it is supported or refuted, researchers need to select a research _____________.

7. A _____________ is a study, generally in the form of an interview or questionnaire, which provides sociologists with information concerning how people think and act.

8. In 1999, Tom Smith analyzed the data from the 1998 General Social Survey focusing on _____________ _____________. After review of the data it was determined that the response rates varied according to how the question was phrased.

9. If scientists were testing a new type of toothpaste, they would administer the toothpaste to a (an) _____________ group, but not to a (an) _____________ group.

10. Researchers can avoid the _____________ effect by conducting secondary analysis.

11. A researcher using census data in a way that was unintended by the initial collectors of that information would be an example of ______________ ______________.

12. Using content analysis, ______________ ______________ conducted a pioneering exploration of how advertisements in 1979 portrayed women as inferior to men.

13. The American Sociological Association's Code of ______________ requires sociologists to maintain objectivity and integrity in research and to preserve the confidentiality of their subjects.

14. As part of their commitment to ______________ neutrality, investigators have an ethical obligation to accept research findings even when the data run counter to their own personal views or widely accepted beliefs.

15. In her book *The Death of White Sociology,* ______________ ______________ called attention to the tendency of mainstream sociology to treat the lives of African Americans as a social problem.

UNDERSTANDING SOCIAL POLICY: All the following questions are based on material that appears in the social policy section on studying human sexuality. Write a brief answer to each question in the space provided below.

1. What research has been done in regard to studying human sexuality?

2. How does the issue of value neutrality relate to studying human sexuality?

3. What attempts have been made to administer a national survey and how did the government respond?

DEFINITIONS OF KEY TERMS

Scientific method: A systematic, organized series of steps that ensures maximum objectivity and consistency in researching a problem. (28)

Operational definition: An explanation of an abstract concept that is specific enough to allow a researcher to measure the concept. (29)

Hypothesis: A speculative statement about the relationship between two or more variables. (30)

Variable: A measurable trait or characteristic that is subject to change under different conditions. (30)

Independent variable: The variable in a causal relationship that, when altered, causes or influences a change in a second variable. (30)

Dependent variable: The variable in a causal relationship that is subject to the influence of another variable. (30)

Causal logic: The relationship between a condition or variable and a particular consequence with one event leading to the other. (30)

Correlation: A relationship between two variables, whereby a change in one coincides with a change in the other. (30)

Representative sample: A selection from a larger population that is statistically found to be typical of that population. (31)

Random sample: A sample for which every member of the entire population has the same chance of being selected. (31)

Validity: The degree to which a scale or measure truly reflects the phenomenon under study. (32)

Reliability: The extent to which a measure provides consistent results. (32)

Control variable: A factor held constant to test the relative impact of an independent variable. (32)

Research design: A detailed plan or method for obtaining data scientifically. (33)

Survey: A study, generally in the form of interviews or questionnaires, which provides sociologists and other researchers with information concerning how people think and act. (33)

Interview: A face-to-face or telephone questioning of a respondent to obtain desired information. (34)

Questionnaire: A printed research instrument employed to obtain desired information from a respondent. (34)

Observation: A research technique in which an investigator collects information through direct participation and/or observation of a group, tribe, or community. (34)

Qualitative research: Research that relies on what is seen in field or naturalistic settings more than on statistical data. (35)

Ethnography: The study of an entire social setting through extended systematic observation. (35)

Quantitative research: Research that collects and reports data primarily in numerical form. (34)

Experiment: An artificially created situation that allows the researcher to manipulate variables. (36)

Experimental group: Subjects in an experiment who are exposed to an independent variable introduced by a researcher. (36)

Control group: Subjects in an experiment who are not introduced to the independent variable by the researchers. (37)

Hawthorne effect: The unintended influence that observers or experiments can have on their subjects. (37)

Secondary analysis: A variety of research techniques that make use of publicly accessible information and data. (37)

Content analysis: The systematic coding and objective recording of data, guided by some rationale. (38)

Code of ethics: The standards of acceptable behavior developed by and for members of a profession. (39)

Value neutrality: Max Weber's term for objectivity of sociologists in the interpretation of data. (40)

ANSWERS TO SELF-TEST

Modified True-False Questions

1. The second step in the scientific method is reviewing the literature. Formulating the hypothesis is the third step in the process. (29)
2. The variable hypothesized to cause or influence another is called the independent variable. The dependent variable "depends" on the influence of the independent variable. (30)
3. The results of such polls reflect nothing more than the views of those who happened to see the television program or hear the radio broadcast and took the time, perhaps at some cost, to register their opinions. (31)
4. After collecting and analyzing data, the researchers come to the final step in the scientific method: they develop the conclusion. (32)
5. The Gallup poll and the Harris poll are among the United States' best-known surveys of opinions. (33)
6. There are two main types of *surveys*: the interview and the questionnaire. (34)
7. True (36)
8. The experimental group is exposed to an independent variable; the control group is not. (37)
9. In the Hawthorne study, worker productivity increased because of the greater attention being paid to them and the novelty of being subjects in an experiment. (37)
10. The most frequently used existing sources in sociological research are census data; crime statistics; and birth, death, marriage, and divorce statistics. (38)
11. The Code of Ethics does not expect researchers to report all illegal behavior to appropriate authorities, which would be a violation of confidentiality, and would destroy the relationship the researcher has with the subject(s). (39)
12. Zellner's research raises questions of unethical practice because he misrepresented the motives of his study and failed to obtain his subjects' informed consent. Zellner's research raised an additional ethical issue: the possibility of harm to those who were interviewed. (40)
13. True (40)
14. Rick Scarce declined to tell a federal grand jury what he knew, or even whether he knew anything about a 1991 raid on a university research library. He was jailed for contempt of court and served 159 days in jail. (40)
15. True (40)

Multiple-Choice Questions

1. b (29)
2. c (30)
3. b (30)
4. c (31)
5. c (33)
6. a (33)
7. a (34)
8. b (35)
9. a (36)
10. c (37)
11. c (37)
12. d (38)
13. d (39)
14. d (40)
15. a (46)

Fill-In Questions

1. scientific (28)
2. literature (29)
3. hypothesis (30)
4. variables (30)
5. independent (30)
6. design (33)
7. survey (33)
8. interracial friendships (35)
9. experimental; control (37)
10. Hawthorne (37)

11. secondary analysis (37)
12. Erving Goffman (38)
13. Ethics (39)
14. value (40)
15. Joyce Ladner (41)

UNDERSTANDING SOCIAL POLICY: Studying Human Sexuality

1. We have little reliable data on patterns of sexual behavior in the United States. Until recently, the only comprehensive study of sexual behavior was the famous two-volume Kinsey Report prepared in the 1940s. The volunteers interviewed for the report were not representative of the nation's adult population. In part, we have little reliable data on patterns of sexual behavior because it is difficult for researchers to obtain accurate information about this sensitive subject. Moreover, until AIDS emerged in the 1980s, there was little scientific demand for data on sexual behavior, except for specific areas such as contraception. (43)
2. The controversy surrounding research on human sexual behavior raises the issue of value neutrality. This becomes especially delicate when one considers the relationship of sociology to the government. The federal government has become the major source of funding for sociological research. Yet Max Weber urged that sociology remain an autonomous discipline and not become unduly influenced by any one segment of society. Conflict theorists and feminists, among others, are critical of some research that claims to be objective. (44)
3. In 1987 the National Institute of Child Health and Human Development sought proposals for a national survey of sexual behavior. However, in 1991, led by Senator Jesse Helms and other conservatives, the U.S. Senate voted 66–34 to forbid funding any survey on adult sexual practices. Helms appealed to popular fears by arguing that such surveys of sexual behavior were intended to "legitimize homosexual lifestyles," and to support "sexual decadence." (45)

CHAPTER 3 CULTURE

KEY POINTS

Culture and Society: **Culture** is the totality of learned, socially transmitted behavior. It includes the ideas, values, customs, and artifacts (for example, CDs, comic books, and birth control devices) of groups of people. A fairly large number of people are said to constitute a **society** when they live in the same territory, are relatively independent of people outside their area, and participate in a common culture. Members of a society generally share a common language, which facilitates day-to-day exchanges with others. (51)

Cultural Universals: Despite their differences, all societies have developed certain common practices and beliefs known as **cultural universals**. Anthropologist George Murdock compiled a list of cultural universals, including athletic sports, cooking, funeral ceremonies, medicine, and sexual restrictions. The cultural practices listed by Murdock may be universal, but the manner in which they are expressed varies from culture to culture. (52)

Material and Nonmaterial Culture: Sociologist William F. Ogburn made a useful distinction between the elements of **material** and **nonmaterial culture**. Material culture refers to the physical or technological aspects of our daily lives, including food items, houses, factories, and raw materials. Nonmaterial culture refers to ways of using material objects, and to customs, beliefs, philosophies, governments, and patterns of communication. Generally, the nonmaterial culture is more resistant to change than is the material culture. (54)

Language: **Language** is an abstract system of word meanings and symbols for all aspects of culture. It includes speech, written characters, numerals, symbols, and gestures and expressions of nonverbal communication. Unlike some other elements of culture, language permeates all parts of society. While language is a cultural universal, striking differences in the use of language are evident around the world. (55)

Norms: Norms are established standards of behavior maintained by a society. **Formal norms** have generally been written down and specify strict rules for punishment of violators. By contrast, **informal norms** are generally understood, but are not precisely recorded. **Mores** are norms deemed highly necessary to the welfare of a society often because they embody the most cherished principles of a people. **Folkways** are norms governing everyday behavior. Society is less likely to formalize folkways than mores, and their violation raises comparatively little concern. (58)

Sanctions: **Sanctions** are penalties and rewards for conduct concerning a social norm. Conformity to a norm can lead to positive sanctions such as a pay raise, a medal, a word of gratitude, or a pat on the back. Negative sanctions include fines, threats, imprisonment, and stares of contempt. (59)

Values: Values are collective conceptions of what is considered good, desirable, and proper—or bad, undesirable, and improper—in a culture. Values influence people's behavior and serve as criteria for evaluating the actions of others. There is often a direct relationship among the values, norms, and sanctions of a culture. (60)

Culture and the Dominant Ideology: Functionalists maintain that stability requires consensus and the support of society's members; consequently, there are strong central values and common norms. Conflict theorists agree that a common culture may exist, but they argue that it serves to maintain the privileges of some groups rather than others. The term **dominant ideology** describes the set of cultural beliefs and practices that help to maintain powerful social, economic, and political interests. From a conflict perspective, the dominant ideology has major social significance. Not only do a society's most powerful groups and institutions control wealth and property, perhaps more importantly, they control the means of producing beliefs about reality through religion, education, and the media. (61)

Subcultures: A **subculture** is a segment of society that shares a distinctive pattern of mores, folkways, and values that differ from the patterns of the larger society. The existence of many subcultures is characteristic of complex societies, such as the United States. Members of a subculture participate in the dominant culture, while at the same time engaging in their unique and distinctive forms of behavior. Frequently, a subculture will develop an **argot**, or specialized language, which distinguishes it from the wider society. (61)

Culture Shock: Anyone who feels disoriented, out of place, even fearful, when immersed in an unfamiliar culture may be experiencing **culture shock**. All of us, to some extent, take for granted the cultural practices of our society. As a result, it can be surprising and even disturbing to realize that other cultures do not follow our "way of life." (63)

Ethnocentrism: Sociologist William Graham Sumner coined the term **ethnocentrism** to refer to the tendency to assume that one's own culture and way of life constitute the norm or are superior to all others. The ethnocentric person sees his or her own group as the center or defining point of culture, and views all other cultures as deviations from what is "normal." Conflict theorists point out that ethnocentric value judgments serve to devalue groups and to deny equal opportunities. Functionalists note that ethnocentrism serves to maintain a sense of solidarity by promoting group pride. (63)

Cultural Relativism: While ethnocentrism evaluates foreign cultures using the familiar culture of the observer as a standard of correct behavior, cultural relativism views people's behavior from the perspective of their own culture. It places a priority on understanding other cultures, rather than dismissing them as "strange" or "exotic." Unlike ethnocentrism, cultural relativism employs the kind of value neutrality in scientific study that Max Weber saw as so important. (65)

KEY TERMS

Briefly define or identify the following terms in the spaces provided below. The definitions of these terms can be found later in this chapter of the study guide.

Culture	Culture lag
Society	Language
Cultural universals	Sapir-Whorf hypothesis
Innovation	Norms
Discovery	Formal norms
Invention	Law
Globalization	Informal norms
Diffusion	Mores
Technology	Folkways

Material culture	Sanctions
Nonmaterial culture	Values
Dominant ideology	Ethnocentrism
Subculture	Cultural relativism
Argot	Xenocentrism
Counterculture	Bilingualism
Culture shock	

SELF-TEST

MODIFIED TRUE-FALSE QUESTIONS: If the statement below is true, write "true" in the space provided. If the statement is false, briefly correct the error.

1. In the view of sociologists, a portrait by Rembrandt is an aspect of culture; a portrait of a billboard painter is not.

2. Some of the examples of cultural universals noted in your text are athletic sports, funerals, medicine, and war.

3. There are two forms of innovation: discovery and diffusion.

4. The material culture is more resistant to change than the nonmaterial culture.

5. The Sapir-Whorf hypothesis holds that language is a “given.”

6. The requirements for a college major and the rules of a card game are considered informal norms.

7. Even on clotheslines, mores in Southeast Asia dictate male dominance in that women’s attire is hung lower than that of men.

8. Society is more likely to formalize mores than folkways.

9. Conformity to a norm can lead to positive sanctions.

10. There is often a direct relationship among the values, norms, and sanctions of a culture.

11. From a functionalist perspective, the dominant ideology has major social significance. Not only do a society's most powerful groups and institutions control wealth and property, perhaps more importantly, they control the means of producing beliefs about reality through religion, education, and the family.

12. The feminist perspective argues that the dominant ideology in the United States will help to control women and keep them in a subordinate position.

13. In the wake of the World Trade Center bombings on September 11, 2001, people in the United States learned of the existence of another left-wing counterculture: armed militia.

14. Sociologist Robert Merton coined the term *ethnocentrism* to refer to the tendency to assume that one's own culture and way of life constitute the norm or are superior to all others.

15. Cultural relativism requires that we accept without question every form of behavior characteristic of a culture.

MULTIPLE-CHOICE QUESTIONS: In each of the following, select the phrase that best completes the statement.

1. Which of the following is an aspect of culture?
   a. a comic book
   b. patriotic attachment to the flag of the United States
   c. burial of a family pet in a cemetery plot
   d. all of the above

2. A list of cultural universals was compiled by anthropologist
   a. Max Weber.
   b. George Murdock.
   c. Margaret Mead.
   d. William F. Ogburn.

3. The identification of a new moon of Saturn was an act of
   a. invention.
   b. discovery.
   c. diffusion.
   d. cultural integration.

4. The distinction between elements of material and nonmaterial culture was made by sociologist
   a. Max Weber.
   b. George Murdock.
   c. Margaret Mead.
   d. William F. Ogburn.

5. In its study of language, which sociological perspective focuses on how people rely on shared definitions of phrases and expressions in both formal speech and everyday conversation?
   a. the functionalist perspective
   b. the conflict perspective
   c. the interactionist perspective
   d. the ethnocentric perspective

6. In the United States, we often formalize norms into
   a. folkways.
   b. mores.
   c. values.
   d. laws.

7. Which of the following statements about norms is correct?
   a. People do not follow norms in all situations. In some cases, they evade a norm because they know it is weakly enforced.
   b. In some instances, behavior that appears to violate society's norms may actually represent adherence to the norms of a particular group.
   c. Norms are violated in some instances because one norm conflicts with another.
   d. all of the above

8. Which of the following statements about values is correct?
   a. Values never change.
   b. Values of a culture may change, but most remain relatively stable during any one person's lifetime.
   c. Values are constantly changing; sociologists view them as being very unstable.
   d. all of the above

9. Which sociological perspective argues that a common culture serves to maintain the privileges of some groups while keeping others in a subservient position?
   a. the functionalist perspective
   b. the conflict perspective
   c. the interactionist perspective
   d. all of the above

10. Which of the following argued that a capitalist society has a dominant ideology that serves the interests of the ruling class?
    a. Max Weber
    b. Talcott Parsons
    c. Karl Marx
    d. Margaret Mead

11. Older people living in housing for the elderly, workers in an offshore oil rig, rodeo cowboys, and circus performers are all examples of what sociologists refer to as
    a. subcultures.
    b. countercultures.
    c. cultural universals.
    d. argot.

12. While vacationing in Great Britain, you discover that the British drive on the "wrong" side of the road, are critical of your United States accent, and will not accept dollars in stores. You feel disoriented and out of place. You are experiencing
    a. xenocentrism.
    b. the Hawthorne effect.
    c. the Sapir-Whorf hypothesis.
    d. culture shock.

13. The term *ethnocentrism* was coined by sociologist
    a. William F. Ogburn.
    b. William Graham Sumner.
    c. George Murdock.
    d. Max Weber.

14. Which sociological perspective emphasizes that ethnocentrism serves to maintain a sense of solidarity by promoting group pride?
    a. the functionalist perspective
    b. the conflict perspective
    c. the interactionist perspective
    d. the dramaturgical perspective

15. In a sense, xenocentrism is a reverse form of
    a. cultural integration.
    b. cultural relativism.
    c. ethnocentrism.
    d. culture shock.

FILL-IN QUESTIONS: Fill in the blank spaces in the sentences below with the correct words. Where two or more words are required, there will be a corresponding number of blank spaces.

1. A ______________ is the largest form of human group.

2. As the number of discoveries in a culture increase, ______________ become possible.

3. Even within a society, ______________ occurs as innovation, discoveries, and inventions gain wider acceptance.

4. Language does more than describe reality; it also serves to ______________ the reality of a culture.

5. "Put on some clean clothes for dinner," and "thou shalt not kill" are both examples of ______________ found in our culture.

6. The United States has strong ______________ against murder, treason, and child abuse that have been institutionalized into formal norms.

7. As support for traditional norms weakens, people will feel free to violate them more frequently and openly, and will be less likely to receive serious negative ______________ for doing so.

8. During the 1980s and 1990s, there was growing support for values having to do with ______________, power, and status.

9. From the ______________ perspective, the dominant ideology has major social significance. Not only do a society's most powerful groups and institutions control wealth and property, perhaps more importantly, they control the means of producing beliefs about reality through religion, education, and the media.

10. Sociologists associated with the ______________ perspective emphasize that language and symbols offer a powerful way for a subculture to maintain its identity.

11. Countercultures are typically popular among the ______________, who have the least investment in the existing culture.

12. Hippies can be viewed as an example of a ______________.

13. The ______________ approach to social behavior points out that ethnocentric value judgments serve to devalue groups and contribute to denial of equal opportunities.

14. Cultural relativism places a priority on ______________ other cultures rather than dismissing them as "strange" or "exotic."

15. People in the United States who automatically assume that French fashions or Japanese electronic devices are superior to our own are engaging in ______________.

UNDERSTANDING SOCIAL POLICY: All the following questions are based on material that appears in the social policy section on bilingualism. Write a brief answer to each question in the space provided below.

1. What is bilingualism?

2. What is the functionalist view of bilingualism and what is the problem with this approach?

3. What is the conflict view of bilingualism?

4. What are the two major areas in which bilingualism has policy implications?

DEFINITIONS OF KEY TERMS

Culture: The totality of learned behavior. (51)
Society: A fairly large number of people who live in the same territory, are relatively independent of people outside it, and participate in a common culture. (51)
Cultural universals: General practices found in every culture. (52)
Innovation: The process of introducing new elements into a culture through either discovery or invention. (52)
Discovery: The process of making known or sharing the existence of an aspect of reality. (53)
Invention: The combination of existing cultural items into a form that did not previously exist. (53)
Globalization: The worldwide integration of government policies, cultures, social movements, and financial markets through trade and the exchange of ideas. (53)
Diffusion: The process by which a cultural item is spread from group to group, or from society to society. (53)
Technology: Information about how to use the material resources of the environment to satisfy human needs and desires. (54)
Material culture: The physical or technological aspects of our daily lives. (54)

Nonmaterial culture: Cultural adjustments to material conditions, such as customs, beliefs, patterns of communication, and ways of using material objects. (54)

Culture lag: Ogburn's term for a period of maladjustment during which the nonmaterial culture is still adapting to new material conditions. (55)

Language: An abstract system of word meanings and symbols for all aspects of culture. It also includes gestures and other nonverbal communication. (55)

Sapir-Whorf hypothesis: A hypothesis concerning the role of language in shaping cultures. It holds that language is culturally determined and serves to influence our mode of thought. (56)

Norms: Established standards of behavior maintained by a society. (58)

Formal norms: Norms that have generally been written down, and that specify strict rules for punishment of violators. (58)

Law: Governmental social control. (58)

Informal norms: Norms that are generally understood, but that are not precisely recorded. (58)

Mores: Norms deemed highly necessary to the welfare of a society. (58)

Folkways: Norms governing everyday social behavior whose violation raises comparatively little concern. (58)

Sanctions: Penalties and rewards for conduct concerning a social norm. (59)

Values: Collective conceptions of what is considered good, desirable, and proper—or bad, undesirable, and improper—in a culture. (60)

Dominant ideology: A set of cultural beliefs and practices that help maintain powerful social, economic, and political interests. (61)

Subculture: A segment of society that shares a distinctive pattern of mores, folkways, and values that differ from the pattern of the larger society. (61)

Argot: Specialized language used by members of a group or subculture. (62)

Counterculture: A subculture that deliberately opposes certain aspects of the larger culture. (63)

Culture shock: The feeling of surprise and disorientation that is experienced when people witness cultural practices different from their own. (63)

Ethnocentrism: The tendency to assume that one's culture and way of life represent the norm, or is superior to all others. (63)

Cultural relativism: The viewing of people's behavior from the perspective of their own culture. (65)

Xenocentrism: The belief that the products, styles, or ideas of one's society are inferior to those that originate elsewhere. (65)

Bilingualism: The use of two or more languages in particular settings, such as workplaces or educational facilities, and the treatment of each language as equally legitimate. (65)

ANSWERS TO SELF-TEST

Modified True-False Questions

1. Sociologists consider both a portrait by Rembrandt and a portrait by a billboard painter to be aspects of culture. (51)
2. Athletic sports, funerals, and medicine are on the list of cultural universals developed by George Murdock, but war is not. (52)
3. There are two forms of innovation: discovery and invention. (53)
4. Generally, the nonmaterial culture is more resistant to change than is the material culture. (54)
5. The Sapir-Whorf hypothesis holds that language is not a "given." (56)
6. The requirements for a college major and the rules of a card game are considered formal norms. (58)
7. Even on clotheslines in Southeast Asia, *folkways* dictate male dominance: women's attire is hung lower than that of men. (58)
8. True (58)
9. True (59)
10. True (60)
11. From a conflict perspective, the dominant ideology has major social significance. Not only do a society's most powerful groups and institutions control wealth and property, more importantly, they control the means of producing beliefs about reality through religion, education, and the media. (61)
12. True (61)
13. In the wake of the World Trade Center bombing on September 11, 2001, people in the United States learned of terrorist groups operating as a counterculture within their country. (63)
14. Sociologist William Graham Sumner coined the term *ethnocentrism* to refer to the tendency to assume that one's own culture and way of life constitute the norm or are superior to all others. (63)
15. While cultural relativism does not suggest that we must accept without question every form of behavior characteristic of a culture, it does require a serious and unbiased effort to evaluate norms, values, and customs in light of the distinctive culture of which they are a part. (65)

Multiple-Choice Questions

1. d (51)
2. b (52)
3. b (53)
4. d (54)
5. c (56)
6. d (58)
7. d (58)
8. b (60)
9. b (61)
10. c (61)
11. a (61)
12. d (63)
13. b (63)
14. a (64)
15. c (65)

Fill-In Questions:

1. society (51)
2. inventions (53)
3. diffusion (53)
4. shape (56)
5. norms (58)
6. mores (58)
7. sanctions (59)
8. money (61)
9. conflict (61)
10. interactionist (62)
11. young (63)
12. counterculture (63)
13. conflict (64)
14. understanding (65)
15. xenocentrism (65)

UNDERSTANDING SOCIAL POLICY: Bilingualism

1. Bilingualism refers to the use of two or more languages in a particular setting, such as the workplace or educational facilities, and the treatment of each language as equally legitimate. Thus, a program of bilingual education may instruct children in their native language while gradually introducing them to the language of the host society. If the curriculum is also bicultural, it will teach children about the mores and folkways of both the dominant culture and the subculture. (65)
2. For a long time, people in the United States demanded conformity to a single language. In a sense, this demand coincides with the functionalist view that language serves to unify members of a society. In some cases, immigrant children were actually forbidden to speak their native languages on school grounds. There was little respect granted to immigrants' cultural traditions. (66)
3. Conflict theory helps us understand some of the attacks on bilingual programs. Many of the attacks stem from an ethnocentric point of view, which hold that any deviation from the majority is bad. This attitude tends to be expressed by those who wish to stamp out foreign influence wherever it occurs, especially in our schools. (66)
4. Bilingualism has policy implications largely in two areas: (1) efforts to maintain language purity, and (2) programs to enhance bilingual education. Nations vary dramatically in their tolerance for a variety of languages. Policy makers in the United States have been somewhat ambivalent in dealing with the issue of bilingualism. In 1965, the Elementary and Secondary Education Act (ESEA) provided for bilingual, bicultural education. Then, in the 1970s, the federal government took an active role in establishing the proper form for bilingual programs. However, more recently, federal policy has been less supportive of bilingualism. Local school districts have been forced to provide an increased share of funding for their bilingual programs. (66)

CHAPTER 4

SOCIALIZATION

The Role of Socialization
- *Environment: The Impact of Isolation*
- *The Influence of Heredity*
- *Sociobiology*

The Self and Socialization
- *Sociological Approaches to the Self*
- *Psychological Approaches to the Self*

Socialization and the Life Course
- *The Life Course*
- *Anticipatory Socialization and Resocialization*

Agents of Socialization
- *Family*
- *School*
- *Peer Group*
- *Mass Media and Technology*
- *Workplace*
- *The State*

Social Policy and Socialization: Child Care around the World
- *The Issue*
- *The Setting*
- *Sociological Insights*
- *Policy Initiatives*

BOXES
- ***SOCIOLOGY IN THE GLOBAL COMMUNITY:*** *Raising Amish Children*
- ***RESEARCH IN ACTION:*** *Impression Management by Students After Exams*

KEY POINTS

Socialization: **Socialization** is the process whereby people learn the attitudes, values, and actions appropriate to individuals as members of a particular culture. From a microsociological perspective, socialization helps us discover how to behave properly, and what to expect from others if we follow (or challenge) society's norms and values. From a macrosociological perspective, socialization provides for the transmission of a culture from one generation to the next, and thereby for the long-term continuance of a society. (73)

Nature versus Nurture: Researchers have traditionally clashed over the relative importance of biological inheritance and environmental factors in human development. This conflict has been called the nature versus nurture (or heredity versus environment) debate. Today, most social scientists have moved beyond this debate, acknowledging instead the interaction of these variables in shaping human development. (73)

Sociobiology: **Sociobiology** is the systematic study of the biological bases of social behavior. Sociobiologists basically apply naturalist Charles Darwin's principles of **natural selection** to the study of social behavior. In its extreme form, sociobiology suggests that all behavior is the result of genetic or biological factors, and that social interactions play no role in shaping people's conduct. (76)

Cooley and the Looking-Glass Self: In the early 1900s, Charles Horton Cooley advanced the belief that we learn who we are by interacting with others. Cooley used the phrase **looking-glass self** to emphasize that the self is the product of our social interactions with other people. A subtle but critical aspect of Cooley's looking-glass self is that the self results from an individual's "imagination" of how others view him or her. (76)

Mead—Stages of the Self: George Herbert Mead continued Cooley's exploration of interactionist theory. Mead developed a useful model of the process by which the self emerges, which is defined by three distinct states. During the preparatory stage, children merely imitate the people around them, especially family members with whom they continually interact. During the play stage, the child becomes able to pretend to be other people. Just as an actor "becomes" a character, a child becomes a doctor, parent, superhero, or ship captain. Finally, in the game stage, the child of about eight or nine years old no longer just plays roles but begins to consider several actual tasks and relationships simultaneously. (77)

Goffman—Presentation of the Self: Early in life, the individual learns to slant his or her presentation of the self in order to create distinctive appearances and to satisfy particular audiences. Erving Goffman refers to this altering of the presentation of the self as

impression management. He makes so many explicit parallels to the theatrical stage that his view has been termed the **dramaturgical approach**. According to this perspective, people resemble performers in action. (78)

Anticipatory Socialization and Resocialization: **Anticipatory socialization** refers to the processes of socialization in which a person "rehearses" for future positions, occupations, and social relationships. Occasionally, assuming new social and occupational positions requires us to unlearn a previous orientation. **Resocialization** refers to the process of discarding former behavior patterns and accepting new ones as part of a transition in one's life. (81)

Total Institutions: Erving Goffman coined the term **total institutions** to refer to institutions, such as prisons, the military, mental hospitals, and convents that regulate all aspects of a person's life under a single authority. Because the total institution is generally cut off from the rest of society, it provides for all the needs of its members. The individual becomes secondary and rather invisible in the overbearing social environment. (82)

The Family as an Agent of Socialization: The **family** is the most important **agent of socialization** in the United States. Obviously, one of its primary functions is the care and rearing of children. The lifelong process of socialization begins shortly after birth. An infant enters an organized society, becomes part of a generation, and typically enters into a family. As the primary agents of socialization, parents play a critical role in guiding children into those gender roles deemed appropriate in a society. (82)

Schools as an Agent of Socialization: Like the family, **schools** have an explicit mandate to socialize people in the United States, and especially children, into the norms and values of our culture. Functionalists point out that as agents of socialization, schools fulfill the function of teaching the values and customs of the larger society. Conflict theorists agree, but add that schools can reinforce the divisive aspects of society, especially those of social class. (84)

Mass Media and Technology as an Agent of Socialization: In the last 80 years, media innovations—radio, motion pictures, recorded music, television, and the Internet—have become important agents of socialization. Television, in particular, is a critical force in the socialization of children in the United States. Television has certain characteristics that distinguish it from the other agents of socialization. It permits imitation and role-playing but does not encourage more complex forms of learning. Issues have been raised regarding the content of television, popular music, music videos, motion pictures, and Internet websites. These forms of entertainment serve as powerful agents of socialization for many young people in the United States and elsewhere. (86)

The Workplace as an Agent of Socialization: Learning to behave appropriately within an occupation is a fundamental aspect of human socialization. More and more young people work today. Some believe the increasing number of teenagers working earlier in life and for longer hours are now finding the workplace almost as important an agent of socialization as school. Socialization in the workplace becomes different when it involves a more permanent shift from an after-school job to full-time employment. (86)

The State as an Agent of Socialization: Social scientists have increasingly recognized the importance of the **state as an agent of socialization** because of its growing impact on the life course. Traditionally, family members have served as the primary caregivers in our culture, but in the twentieth century, the family's protective function has steadily been transferred to outside agencies such as hospitals, mental health clinics, and insurance companies. The state runs many of these agencies, or licenses and regulates them. (87)

Child Care around the World: Day care centers have become the functional equivalent of the nuclear family, performing some of the nurturing and socialization functions previously handled only by family members. Researchers have found that high-quality child care centers do not adversely affect the socialization of children; in fact, good day care benefits children. Viewed from a conflict perspective, child care costs are an especially serious burden for lower class families, who already find it hard to take advantage of limited job opportunities. Feminists suggest that high-quality child care receives little governmental support because it is regarded as "merely a way to let women work." (88)

KEY TERMS

Briefly define or identify the following terms in the spaces provided below. The definitions of these terms can be found later in this chapter of the study guide.

Socialization	Symbols
Personality	Role taking
Sociobiology	Generalized others
Self	Significant others

Looking-glass self	Impression management
Dramaturgical approach	Resocialization
Face-work	Total institutions
Cognitive theory of development	Degradation ceremony
Rites of passage	Gender roles
Anticipatory socialization	

SELF-TEST

MODIFIED TRUE-FALSE QUESTIONS: If the statement below is true, write "true" in the space provided. If the statement is false, briefly correct the error.

1. Harry Harlow's study of Isabelle, who was raised in social isolation, supports the importance of socialization on development.

2. In its extreme form, sociobiology suggests that social interactions play a significant role in shaping people's conduct.

3. Charles Horton Cooley was a pioneer of the interactionist approach.

4. The "self" is a distinct identity that forms early in life and remains relatively unchanged as we age.

5. During the preparatory stage identified by George Herbert Mead, children become skilled in role taking.

6. As both Charles Horton Cooley and Margaret Mead noted, the development of the self is a critical aspect of the early years of one's life.

7. There appear to be striking differences in whom African Americans and Whites from similar economic backgrounds regard as their significant others.

8. Sociologists Daniel Albas and Cheryl Albas found that students' impression-management strategies are constrained by society's informal norms regarding modesty and consideration for less successful peers.

9. Upon entering prison to begin "doing time," a person may experience the humiliation of a degradation ceremony as he or she is stripped of clothing, jewelry, and other personal possessions.

10. The Amish way of life has changed very little since this group began arriving in the United States during the eighteenth and nineteenth centuries.

11. A report by the American Association of University Women shows that teachers praise boys more than girls, offer boys more academic assistance, and praise boys for the neatness of their work.

12. In general television is a negative socializing influence.

13. Researchers are finding that families are socialized into multitasking as the social norm; devoting one's full attention to one task—even eating or driving—is less common on a typical day.

14. Some observers feel that the increasing number of teenagers who are working earlier in life and for longer hours are now finding the workplace almost as important an agent of socialization as school.

15. The state has had a noteworthy impact on the life course by abolishing traditional rites of passage.

MULTIPLE-CHOICE QUESTIONS: In each of the following, select the phrase that best completes the statement.

1. Isabelle was
   a. reared in an interracial family.
   b. kept in almost total seclusion for the first six years of her life.
   c. subjected to mistreatment in a mental institution.
   d. a child whose language skills were of genius caliber.

2. Harry Harlow conducted a study of
   a. Isabelle and the impact of social isolation on the socialization process.
   b. Nell and the impact of social isolation on the socialization process.
   c. rhesus monkeys that had been raised away from their mothers.
   d. nature versus nurture that focused on sociobiology.

3. Which of the following used the phrase looking-glass self to emphasize that the self is the product of our social interactions with other people?
   a. George Herbert Mead
   b. Charles Horton Cooley
   c. Erving Goffman
   d. Harry Harlow

4. Which sociologist distinguished between significant others and generalized others?
   a. George Herbert Mead
   b. Charles Horton Cooley
   c. Erving Goffman
   d. W.I. Thomas

5. In studying the strategies that college students employ to create desired appearances after grades have been awarded, sociologists Daniel Albas and Cheryl Albas drew upon the concept of impression management developed by
   a. George Herbert Mead.
   b. Charles Horton Cooley.
   c. Erving Goffman.
   d. Jean Piaget.

6. A person does poorly on a college chemistry test and later tells a friend, "The exam wasn't fair! There were trick questions and it covered material that we weren't assigned!" This is an example of
   a. reverse socialization.
   b. face-work.
   c. studied nonobservance.
   d. anticipatory socialization.

7. Jean Piaget found that although newborns have no self in the sense of a looking-glass image, they are quite
   a. ethnocentric.
   b. self-centered.
   c. other-directed.
   d. deterministic.

8. Which of the following is an example of a rite of passage?
   a. school graduation
   b. marriage
   c. retirement
   d. all of the above

9. Which of the following is considered a total institution?
   a. a university
   b. a mental hospital
   c. a factory
   d. all of the above

10. On the first day of basic training in the army, a recruit has his civilian clothes replaced with army "greens," has his hair shaved off, loses his privacy, and finds that he must use a communal bathroom. All of these humiliating activities are part of a (an)
   a. significant other.
   b. impression management.
   c. degradation ceremony.
   d. face-work.

11. The institution most closely associated with the process of socialization is the
   a. family.
   b. peer group.
   c. school.
   d. state.

12. The term gender role refers to
    a. the biological fact that we are male or female.
    b. a role that is given to us by a teacher.
    c. a role that is given to us in a play.
    d. expectations regarding the proper behavior, attitudes, and activities of males and females.

13. Which sociological perspective emphasizes that schools in the United States foster competition through built-in systems of reward and punishment?
    a. the functionalist perspective
    b. the conflict perspective
    c. the interactionist perspective
    d. the psychological perspective

14. In the twentieth century, the family's protective function has increasingly been transferred to outside agencies, such as
    a. hospitals.
    b. mental health clinics.
    c. insurance companies.
    d. all of the above

15. The state has had a noteworthy impact on the life course by re-instituting the rites of passage that had disappeared in agricultural societies and in periods of early industrialization. An example of this is
    a. the driving age.
    b. the legal drinking age.
    c. parental permission to marry.
    d. all of the above

FILL-IN QUESTIONS: Fill in the blank spaces in the sentences below with the correct words. Where two or more words are required, there will be a corresponding number of blank spaces.

1. _______________ affects the overall cultural practices of a society, and it also shapes the image that we hold of ourselves.

2. Sociobiologists basically apply the principles of natural selection developed by _______________ _______________ to the study of social behavior.

3. ______________ theorists fear that the sociobiological approach could be used as an argument against efforts to assist disadvantaged people, such as schoolchildren who are not competing successfully.

4. Mead referred to those people who play a major role in shaping a person's identity, such as parents, friends, coworkers, coaches, and teachers, as ______________ others.

5. A waiter may "not see" a customer who wants more coffee. Sociologist ______________ ______________ examined such behavior using the dramaturgical approach.

6. Early work in ______________, such as that of Sigmund Freud, stressed the role of inborn drives—among them the drive for sexual gratification—in channeling human behavior.

7. The first stage in Jean Piaget's well-known cognitive theory of development is the ______________ stage, when children first discover that their hands are actually part of themselves.

8. Preparation for many aspects of adult life begins with ______________ socialization during childhood and adolescence, and continues throughout our lives as we prepare for new responsibilities.

9. Resocialization is particularly effective when it occurs within a ______________ institution.

10. Amish youth often go through a period of discovery called ______________, a term that means "running around."

11. Traditional ______________ roles include men being "tough" and women being "tender."

12. The ______________ perspective reminds us that socialization concerning not only masculinity and femininity, but also marriage and parenthood, begins in childhood as a part of family life.

13. The ______________ perspective of sociology emphasizes the role of schools in teaching the values and customs of the larger society.

14. Children's media usage shows that young people in the United States spend ______________ hours per day with some form of media, mostly television.

15. By regulating the life course to some degree, the _____________ shapes the socialization process by influencing our views of appropriate behavior at particular ages.

UNDERSTANDING SOCIAL POLICY: All the following questions are based on material that appears in the social policy section on day care. Write a brief answer to each question in the space provided below.

1. According to studies, what is the effect of day care on children?

2. What are the conflict and feminist concerns about day care?

3. Why is the turnover of teaching personnel so high in day care centers?

4. What is the difference in day care between developing nations and European nations?

DEFINITIONS OF KEY TERMS

Socialization: The process whereby people learn the attitudes, values, and actions appropriate to individuals as members of a particular culture. (73)

Personality: In everyday speech, a person's typical patterns of attitudes, needs, characteristics, and behavior. (73)

Sociobiology: The systematic study of the biological bases of social behavior. (76)

Self: According to George Herbert Mead, the sum total of people's conscious perception of their identity as distinct from others. (76)

Looking-glass self: A phrase used by Charles Horton Cooley to emphasize that the self is the product of our social interactions with others. (76)

Symbols: The gestures, objects, and language that form the basis of human communication. (77)

Role taking: The process of mentally assuming the perspective of another, thereby enabling one to respond from that imagined viewpoint. (77)

Generalized others: A term used by George Herbert Mead to refer to the child's awareness of the attitudes, viewpoints, and expectations of society as a whole. (77)

Significant others: A term used by George Herbert Mead to refer to those individuals who are most important in the development of the self, such as parents, friends, and teachers. (78)

Impression management: A term used by Erving Goffman to refer to the altering of the presentation of the self in order to create distinctive appearances and satisfy particular others. (78)

Dramaturgical approach: A view of social interaction, popularized by Erving Goffman, under which people are examined as if they were theatrical performers. (78)

Face-work: A term used by Erving Goffman to refer to people's efforts to maintain the proper image and avoid embarrassment in public. (78)

Cognitive theory of development: Jean Piaget's theory explaining how children's thought progresses through four stages. (80)

Rites of passage: Rituals marking the symbolic transition from one social position to another. (80)

Anticipatory socialization: Processes of socialization in which a person "rehearses" for future positions, occupations, and social relationships. (81)

Resocialization: The process of discarding former behavior patterns and accepting new ones as part of a transition in one's life. (82)

Total institutions: A term coined by Erving Goffman to refer to institutions that regulate all aspects of a person's life under a single authority such as prisons, the military, mental hospitals, and convents. (82)

Degradation ceremony: An aspect of the socialization process within total institutions in which people are subjected to humiliating rituals. (82)

Gender roles: Expectations regarding the proper behavior, attitudes, and activities of males and females. (83)

ANSWERS TO SELF-TEST

Modified True-False Questions

1. Harry Harlow studied social isolation using rhesus monkeys. (75)
2. In its extreme form, sociobiology resembles biological determinism by suggesting that all behavior is totally the result of genetic or biological factors. (76)
3. True (76)
4. The self continues to develop and change throughout our lives. (76)
5. During the preparatory stage identified by George Herbert Mead, children merely imitate the people around them. Role taking occurs during the play stage. (77)
6. Cooley and George Herbert Mead (no relation to Margaret Mead) focused on the development and importance of the self. (77)
7. There appears to be little difference in whom African Americans and Whites from similar backgrounds regard as their significant others. (78)
8. True (79)
9. True (82)
10. True (83)
11. The report by the American Association of University Women notes that boys are praised for the intellectual content of their answers, and girls are praised for neatness. (85)
12. Television can be a positive influence: it can introduce children to unfamiliar lifestyles and cultures. (86)
13. True (86)
14. True (86)
15. The state has had a noteworthy impact on the life course by re-instituting the rites of passage that had disappeared in agricultural societies and in periods of early industrialization. (87)

Multiple-Choice Questions

1. b (74)
2. c (75)
3. b (76)
4. a (77)
5. c (78)
6. b (78)
7. b (80)
8. d (81)
9. b (82)
10. c (82)
11. a (82)
12. d (83)
13. b (84)
14. d (87)
15. d (87)

Fill-In Questions

1. Socialization (73)
2. Charles Darwin (76)
3. Conflict (76)
4. significant (78)
5. Erving Goffman (78)
6. psychology (79)
7. sensorimotor (80)
8. anticipatory (81)
9. total (82)
10. *rumspringe* (83)
11. gender (83)
12. interactionist (84)
13. functionalist (84)
14. 5.5 (86)
15. state (87)

UNDERSTANDING SOCIAL POLICY: Child Care around the World

1. Studies indicate that the socialization of children placed in high-quality day care centers is not adversely affected by such experiences; in fact, good day care benefits children. It appears from studies that children may be better off in centers with well-trained caregivers than cared for full time by those mothers who are depressed and frustrated because they wish to work outside the home. (88)
2. Conflict theorists and feminists are concerned that parents in wealthy neighborhoods have an easier time finding day care than those in poor or working-class communities, that day care costs are an especially serious burden for lower-class families, that working mothers rather than working fathers are especially likely to bear the burden of day care problems, and that nearly all day care workers are women who find themselves in low-status, minimum wage jobs. (88)
3. Nearly all day care workers are women; many find themselves in low-status, minimum wage jobs. The average salary of child care workers in the United States in 1998 was only $10,710, and there are few fringe benefits. (89)
4. Most developing nations do not have the economic base to provide subsidized child care, whereas a number of European nations, including the Netherlands and Sweden, impose high taxes while providing excellent preschool care at little or no cost. (89)

CHAPTER

5 SOCIAL INTERACTION AND SOCIAL STRUCTURE

KEY POINTS

Social Interaction and Social Structure: Sociologists use the term **social interaction** to refer to the ways in which people respond to one another. **Social structure** refers to the way in which a society is organized into predictable relationships. These concepts are central to sociological study; they focus on how different aspects of behavior are related to one another. (94)

Social Interaction and Reality: The distinctive characteristic of social interactions among people, according to Herbert Blumer, is that "human beings interpret or 'define' each other's actions instead of merely reacting to each other's action." Reality is shaped by our perceptions, evaluations, and definitions. The ability to define social reality reflects a group's power within a society. Indeed, one of the most crucial aspects of the relationship between dominant and subordinate groups is the ability of the dominant or majority group to define a society's values. (94)

Negotiated Order: Negotiations underlie much of our social behavior. Sociologists use the term, **negotiated order**, to underscore the fact that the social order is continually being constructed and altered through negotiations. Negotiated order refers to a social structure that derives its existence from the social interactions through which people define and redefine its character. Negotiation is a cultural universal; all societies provide guidelines or norms in which negotiation takes place. (95)

Statuses: We normally think of a person's "status" as having to do with influence, wealth, and fame. However, sociologists use **status** to refer to any of the full range of socially defined positions within a large group or society—from the lowest to the highest position. Clearly, a person holds more than one status simultaneously. (96)

Ascribed and Achieved Status: An **ascribed status** is "assigned" to a person by society without regard to that person's unique talents or characteristics. Generally, this assignment takes place at birth; thus, a person's racial background, gender, and age are all considered ascribed statuses. Unlike ascribed statuses, an **achieved status** comes to people largely through their own efforts. One must do something to acquire an achieved status—go to school, learn a skill, establish a friendship, or invent a new product. (96)

Social Roles: A social role is a set of expectations for people who occupy a given social position or status. With each distinctive social status, whether ascribed or achieved, comes particular role expectations. Roles are a significant component of social structure. Viewed from a functionalist perspective, roles contribute to a society's stability by enabling members to anticipate the behavior of others and to pattern their own actions accordingly. Yet social roles can also be dysfunctional by restricting people's interaction and relationships. (97)

Groups: In sociological terms, a group is any number of people with similar norms, values, and expectations who regularly and consciously interact. Groups play a vital part in a society's social structure. Much of our social interaction takes place within groups and is influenced by their norms and sanctions. (100)

Social Institutions: The mass media, the government, the economy, the family, and the health care system are all examples of **social institutions** found in our society. Social institutions are organized patterns of beliefs and behavior centered on basic social needs, such as replacing personnel (the family) and preserving order (the government). (103)

Functionalist View of Social Institutions: One way to understand social institutions can be to see how they fulfill essential functions. Social scientists have identified five major tasks, or functional prerequisites, that a society or relatively permanent group must accomplish if it is to survive. These are (1) replacing personnel, (2) teaching new recruits, (3) producing and distributing goods and services, (4) preserving order, and (5) providing and maintaining a sense of purpose. (103)

Conflict View of Social Institutions: While both the functionalist and the conflict perspectives agree that social institutions are organized to meet basic social needs, conflict theorists object to the implication inherent in the functionalist view that the outcome is necessarily efficient and desirable. From a conflict perspective, major institutions help maintain the privileges of the most powerful individuals and groups within a society while contributing to the powerlessness of others. Social institutions also operate in gendered or racist environments, as conflict theorists as well as feminists and interactionists have pointed out. In schools, offices, and governmental institutions, assumptions are made about what people can do that reflect the sexism and racism of the larger society. (104)

Interactionist View of Social Institutions: Interactionist theorists emphasize that our social behavior is conditioned by the roles and statuses that we accept, the groups to which we belong, and the institutions within which we function. (105)

Tönnies's Gemeinschaft and Gesellschaft: According to sociologist Ferdinand Tönnies, the **Gemeinschaft** community is typical of rural life. It is a small community in which people have similar backgrounds and life experiences. By contrast, the **Gesellschaft** is an ideal type characteristic of modern urban life. Most people are strangers and feel little in common with other community residents. Self-interests dominate, and there is generally little consensus concerning values or commitment to the group. (106)

Lenski's Sociocultural Evolution Approach: Sociologist Gerhard Lenski sees human societies as undergoing change according to a dominant pattern, known as sociocultural evolution. This term refers to the "process of change and development in human societies that results from cumulative growth in their stores of cultural information." In Lenski's view, a society's level of technology is critical to the way it is organized. There are three types of pre-industrial societies, which are categorized according to the way in which the social institution of the economy is organized: (1) the hunting-and-gathering society, (2) the horticultural society, and (3) the agrarian society. As the industrial revolution proceeded, a new form of social structure emerged. An industrial society is a society that depends on mechanization to produce its goods and services. Industrial societies relied on new inventions that facilitated agricultural and industrial production and on new sources of energy such as steam. (107)

The AIDS Crisis: The staggering rise of AIDS cases has affected the social structure of the United States in a profound way. The strain on the nation's health care system has been increasingly evident, as hospitals are becoming overwhelmed by the demands of caring for AIDS patients. Fears about AIDS have led to growing discrimination within major social institutions of the United States. Self-help groups, especially in the gay communities of major cities, have been established to care for the sick, educate the healthy, and lobby for more responsive public policies. (109)

KEY TERMS

Briefly define or identify the following terms in the spaces provided below. The definitions of these terms can be found later in this chapter of the study guide.

Social interaction	Master status
Social structure	Social role
Negotiation	Role conflict
Negotiated order	Role strain
Status	Role exit

Ascribed status	Group
Achieved status	Social network
Social institutions	Horticultural society
Gemeinschaft	Agrarian society
Gesellschaft	Industrial society
Sociocultural evolution	Postindustrial society
Technology	Postmodern society
Hunting-and-gathering society	

SELF-TEST

MODIFIED TRUE-FALSE QUESTIONS: If the statement below is true, write "true" in the space provided. If the statement is false, briefly correct the error.

1. The social structure of Zimbardo's mock prison influenced the interactions between the guards and the prisoners.

2. Friends talking over the telephone and co-workers communicating over a computer are engaged in social interaction.

3. The four basic elements of social structure are functions, behaviors, statuses, and social roles.

4. William I. Thomas noted that people respond only to the objective features of a person or situation.

5. Bargaining, compromising, trading off, agreeing, mediating, exchanging, "wheeling and dealing," and collusion are all examples of negotiation.

6. Each person can hold only one status.

7. It is relatively easy to change an ascribed status.

8. With each distinctive social role, whether ascribed or achieved, come particular role expectations. However, actual performance varies from individual to individual.

9. Many people with disabilities find that their status as "disabled" functions as a master status that overshadows their actual ability to perform successfully in meaningful employment.

10. Social roles can be dysfunctional by restricting people's relationships with each other.

11. The last stage of role exit involves the creation of a new identity.

12. In her study of Hispanic women employed as domestic workers, sociologist Pierrette Hondagneu-Sotelo found that these women are isolated from each other since they work alone, and therefore, have not established social networks.

13. According to Talcott Parsons and Robert Merton, the five major tasks or functional prerequisites that a society or relatively permanent group must accomplish if it is to survive are replacing personnel, teaching new recruits, producing and distributing goods and services, preserving order, and providing and maintaining a sense of purpose.

14. Interactionist theorists emphasize that our social behavior is conditioned by the roles and statuses that we accept, the groups to which we belong, and the institutions within which we function.

15. Social change is an important aspect of life in the Gemeinschaft; it can be strikingly evident even within a single generation.

MULTIPLE-CHOICE QUESTIONS: In each of the following, select the phrase that best completes the statement.

1. In Zimbardo's mock prison experiment at Stanford University
   a. the social interactions between the prisoners and the guards influenced the social structure of the prison.
   b. the social structure of the prison influenced the social interactions between the prisoners and the guards.
   c. there was no relationship between social interaction and social structure.
   d. Zimbardo believed that social structure and social interaction influence each other.

2. Which sociologist saw that the "definition of the situation" could mold the thinking and personality of the individual?
   a. Philip Zimbardo
   b. Herbert Blumer
   c. William I. Thomas
   d. Erving Goffman

3. Which of the following statements is not correct?
   a. Sociologists use the term negotiated order to underscore the fact that social order is continually being constructed and altered through negotiation.
   b. Negotiation is a cultural universal.
   c. Most elements of social structure are not static and are therefore subject to change through bargaining and exchanging (negotiation).
   d. Negotiation is a macrolevel process that does not usually involve interactions between small groups, such as families.

4. Which of the following is an ascribed status?
   a. daughter
   b. long-distance runner
   c. doctor
   d. all of the above

5. Which of the following is an achieved status?
   a. senior citizen
   b. member of the female sex
   c. bank robber
   d. Native American

6. It is the fourth week of the semester and your class has decided that Professor Jones is an excellent instructor. Professor Jones is also a disabled middle-aged male. To students in his class, Professor Jones's master status is
   a. excellent instructor.
   b. disabled.
   c. middle-aged.
   d. male.

7. During World War II, Christians living in Nazi Germany had to choose between trying to protect Jewish friends and associates, and turning them in to the authorities. This is an example of
   a. cultural universalism.
   b. role strain.
   c. functional prerequisites.
   d. role conflict.

8. You are a student at XYZ College, and you have your sociology and history final exams on the same morning. You know that preparing for both exams at the same time is going to lead to lower grades in one or both of the exams. The conflict that you are experiencing as you try to fulfill both of your responsibilities at the college is an example of
   a. role conflict.
   b. role exit.
   c. role strain.
   d. role dissonance.

9. Which of the following would experience role exit?
   a. a retired person
   b. a recovering alcoholic
   c. a nun who leaves her religious order
   d. all of the above

10. In sociological terms, which of the following constitutes a group?
   a. members of a hospital's business office
   b. all residents of the state of Vermont
   c. women in the United States over 50
   d. all of the above

11. Which sociological perspective has identified five major tasks that a society must accomplish if it is to survive?
    a. the functionalist perspective
    b. the conflict perspective
    c. the interactionist perspective
    d. the clinical perspective

12. The native people of Tasmania, a large island just south of Australia, are now extinct because they failed to
    a. teach new recruits.
    b. preserve order.
    c. replace personnel.
    d. provide and maintain a sense of purpose.

13. Which sociological perspective emphasizes that the outcome of major social institutions is not necessarily efficient and desirable?
    a. the functionalist perspective
    b. the conflict perspective
    c. the interactionist perspective
    d. all of the above

14. In studying the social behavior of word processors in a Chicago law firm, sociologist Mitchell Duneier drew on the
    a. functionalist perspective.
    b. conflict perspective.
    c. interactionist perspective.
    d. macrosociological perspective.

15. In Gerhard Lenski's theory of sociocultural evolution, a society's level of _______________ is critical to the way it is organized.
    a. agriculture
    b. health care
    c. technology
    d. all of the above

FILL-IN QUESTIONS: Fill in the blank spaces in the sentences below with the correct words. Where two or more words are required, there will be a corresponding number of blank spaces.

1. According to Herbert Blumer, our response to someone's behavior is based on the _______________ we attach to his or her actions.

2. _______________ theorists are especially interested in ascribed statuses, since these statuses often confer privileges or reflect a person's membership in a subordinate group.

3. The African American activist Malcolm X wrote in his autobiography that his position as a Black man (_______________ status) was an obstacle to his dream of becoming a lawyer (_______________ status).

4. With each distinctive social status come particular _______________ expectations.

5. Contemporary sociologists have suggested that society has attached a _______________ to many forms of disability and that this leads to prejudicial treatment.

6. Sociologist Helen Rose Fuchs Ebaugh developed the term _______________ _______________ to describe the process of disengagement from a role that is central to one's self-identity, and re-establishment of an identity in a new role.

7. The mass media, the government, the economy, the family, and the health care system are all examples of _______________ _______________ found in the United States.

8. Teaching of new recruits can take place formally within schools (where learning is a _______________ function) or informally through interaction in peer groups (where instruction is a _______________ function).

9. Viewed from a _______________ perspective, major social institutions help maintain the privileges of the most powerful individuals and groups in a society, while contributing to the powerlessness of others.

10. The concepts of Gemeinschaft and Gesellschaft were developed by German sociologist _______________ _______________.

11. The theory of sociocultural evolution was developed by _______________ _______________.

12. The type of pre-industrial society in which new technological innovations, such as the plow, allowed farmers to dramatically increase their crop yield is called a(n) _____________ society.

13. _____________ societies relied on new inventions that facilitated agricultural and industrial production, and on new sources of energy such as steam.

14. Daniel Bell views the transition from industrial to postindustrial society as a positive development. He sees a rise in interest groups concerned with such national issues as health, education, and the environment. Bell's outlook is _____________ because he portrays postindustrial society as basically consensual.

15. _____________ theorists take a global perspective and note the ways that aspects of culture cross national boundaries.

UNDERSTANDING SOCIAL POLICY: All the following questions are based on material that appears in the social policy section on The AIDS Crisis. Write a brief answer to each question in the space provided below.

1. Why is there such a strong stigma attached to infection with the HIV virus and to AIDS?

2. Viewed from a conflict perspective, why were policymakers slow to respond to the AIDS crisis?

3. What are the two concerns that interactionists have with AIDS that are outlined in the text?

DEFINITIONS OF KEY TERMS

Social interaction: The ways in which people respond to one another. (94)

Social structure: The way in which a society is organized into predictable relationships. (94)

Negotiation: The attempt to reach agreement with others concerning some objective. (95)

Negotiated order: A social structure that derives its existence from the social interactions through which people define and redefine its character. (96)

Status: A term used by sociologists to refer to any of the full range of socially defined positions within a large group or society. (96)

Ascribed status: A social position "assigned" to a person by society without regard for the person's unique talents or characteristics. (96)

Achieved status: A social position attained by a person largely through his or her own effort. (97)

Master status: A status that dominates others and thereby determines a person's general position within society. (97)

Social role: A set of expectations for people who occupy a given social position or status. (97)

Role conflict: Difficulties that occur when incompatible expectations arise from two or more social positions held by the same person. (98)

Role strain: Difficulties that result from the differing demands and expectations associated with the same social position. (99)

Role exit: The process of disengagement from a role that is central to one's self-identity and re-establishment of an identity in a new role. (100)

Group: Any number of people with similar norms, values, and expectations who regularly and consciously interact. (100)

Social network: A series of social relationships that link a person directly to others, and therefore, indirectly to still more people. (101)

Social institutions: Organized patterns of beliefs and behavior centered on basic social needs. (103)

Gemeinschaft: Close-knit communities, often found in rural areas, in which strong personal bonds unite members. (106)

Gesellschaft: Communities, often urban, that are large and impersonal, with little commitment to the group or consensus on values. (107)

Sociocultural evolution: The process of change and development in human societies that results from cumulative growth in their stores of cultural information. (107)

Technology: Information about the ways in which the material resources of the environment may be used to satisfy human needs and desires. (107)

Hunting-and-gathering society: A pre-industrial society in which people rely on whatever foods and fiber are readily available in order to live. (107)

Horticultural society: A pre-industrial society in which people plant seeds and crops rather than subsist merely on available foods. (107)

Agrarian society: The most technologically advanced form of pre-industrial society. Members are primarily engaged in the production of food but increase their crop yield through such innovations as the plow. (107)

Industrial society: A society that depends on mechanization to produce its goods and services. (108)

Postindustrial society: A society whose economic system is primarily engaged in the processing and control of information. (108)

Postmodern society: A technologically sophisticated society that is preoccupied with consumer goods and media images. (108)

ANSWERS TO SELF-TEST

Modified True-False Questions

1. True (94)
2. True (94)
3. The five basic elements of social structure are statuses, social roles, groups, social networks and social institutions. (94)
4. William I. Thomas observed that people respond not only to the objective features of a person or situation, but also to the meaning that the person or situation has for them. (95)
5. Agreeing is not an example of negotiation. (95)
6. A person can hold more than one status simultaneously. (96)
7. In many cases, there is little that people can do to change an ascribed status. (96)
8. True (97)
9. True (97)
10. True (97)
11. True (100)
12. In her study of Hispanic women employed as domestic workers, sociologist Pierrette Hondagneu-Sotelo found that these women have created strong social networks. (102)
13. The five major tasks or functional prerequisites were developed by David F. Aberle, Raymond Mack, and Calvin Bradford. (103)
14. True (105)
15. Social change is an important aspect of life in the Gesellschaft; it can be strikingly evident within a single generation. (107)

Multiple-Choice Questions

1. b (94)
2. c (95)
3. d (95)
4. a (96)
5. c (97)
6. a (97)
7. d (99)
8. c (99)
9. d (100)
10. a (100)
11. a (103)
12. b (103)
13. b (104)
14. c (105)
15. c (107)

Fill-In Questions

1. meaning (94)
2. Conflict (96)
3. ascribed; achieved (96)
4. role (97)
5. stigma (98)
6. role exit (100)
7. social institutions (103)
8. manifest; latent (103)
9. conflict (104)
10. Ferdinand Tönnies (106)
11. Gerhard Lenski (107)
12. agrarian (107)
13. Industrial (108)
14. functionalist (108)
15. Postmodern (108)

UNDERSTANDING SOCIAL POLICY: THE AIDS CRISIS

1. People with AIDS or infected with the HIV virus have faced a powerful dual stigma. Not only are they associated with a lethal and contagious disease, they have a disease that is disproportionately evident in already stigmatized groups, such as gay males and drug users. (110)
2. Viewed from a conflict perspective, policymakers were slow to respond to the AIDS crisis because those in high-risk groups—gay men and IV drug users—are comparatively powerless. Moreover, this linkage with stigmatized groups delayed recognition of the severity of the AIDS epidemic, and the media took little interest in the disease until it seemed to be spreading beyond the gay community. (110)
3. On the microlevel of social interaction, observers widely forecast that AIDS would lead to a more conservative sexual climate among both homosexuals and heterosexuals; one in which people would be much more cautious about involvement with new partners. Another interactionist concern is the tremendous impact on one's daily routine of taking the appropriate medication. (110)

CHAPTER

6 GROUPS AND ORGANIZATIONS

KEY POINTS

Understanding Groups: A **group** is any number of people with similar norms, values, and expectations who regularly and consciously interact. College sororities and fraternities, dance companies, tenants' associations, and chess clubs are all considered examples of groups. The study of groups has become an important part of sociological investigation because they play such a key role in the transmission of culture. (117)

Primary and Secondary Groups: Sociologist Charles Horton Cooley coined the term **primary group** to refer to small groups characterized by intimate, face-to-face association and cooperation. When we find ourselves identifying closely with a group, it is probably a primary group. However, people in the United States participate in many groups that are not characterized by close bonds of friendship, such as large classes and business associations. The term **secondary group** refers to formal, impersonal groups in which there is little social intimacy or mutual understanding. (117)

In-Groups, Out-Groups, and Reference Groups: **In-groups** are groups or categories to which people feel they belong, and **out-groups** are groups or categories to which people feel they do not belong. Sociologists use the term **reference groups** when speaking of any group that individuals use as a standard for evaluating themselves and their own behavior. Reference groups have two basic purposes: (1) they serve a normative function by setting and enforcing standards of conduct and belief; (2) they also perform a comparison function by serving as a standard against which people can measure themselves and others. (118)

Studying Small Groups: The term **small group** is used to refer to a group small enough for all members to interact simultaneously; that is, to talk with one another or at least be acquainted. We may think of small groups as being informal and unpatterned; yet, interactionist researchers have revealed that there are distinct and predictable processes at work in the functioning of small groups. (120)

Formal Organizations: As contemporary societies have shifted to more advanced forms of technology and their social structures have become more complex, our lives have become increasingly dominated by large secondary groups referred to as **formal organizations**. A formal organization is a special-purpose group designed and structured for maximum efficiency. The U.S. Postal Service, the Boston Pops orchestra, and the college you attend are all examples of formal organizations. In our society, formal organizations fulfill an enormous variety of personal and societal needs and shape the lives of every one of us. (121)

Characteristics of a Bureaucracy: A **bureaucracy** is a component of formal organizations in which rules and hierarchical ranking are used to achieve efficiency.

Elements of bureaucracy are found in almost every occupation in an industrial society, such as the United States. Max Weber first directed researchers to the significance of bureaucratic structure. For analytical purposes, he developed an ideal type of bureaucracy that would reflect the most characteristic aspects of all human organizations. He argued that every bureaucracy will have five basic characteristics: division of labor, hierarchy of authority, written rules and regulations, impersonality, and employment based on technical qualifications. (122)

Bureaucratization as a Process: Sociologists have used the term bureaucratization to refer to the process by which a group, organization, or social movement becomes increasingly bureaucratic. Normally, we think of bureaucratization in terms of large organizations. Interestingly, bureaucratization also takes place within small-group settings. (126)

The Iron Law of Oligarchy: German sociologist Robert Michels studied socialist parties and labor unions in Europe before World War I, and found that such organizations were becoming increasingly bureaucratic. Michels originated the idea of the **iron law of oligarchy**, under which a democratic organization will develop into a bureaucracy ruled by a few (the oligarchy). Michels argues that members of an oligarchy are strongly motivated to maintain their leadership roles, privileges, and power. (126)

Bureaucracy and Organizational Culture: How does bureaucratization affect the average individual who works in an organization? According to the classical theory of formal organizations, also known as the scientific management approach, workers are motivated almost entirely by economic rewards. The human relations approach emphasizes the role of people, communication, and participation within a bureaucracy. (126)

Voluntary Associations: **Voluntary associations** are organizations established on the basis of common interest, whose members volunteer or even pay to participate. The Girl Scouts of America, the American Jewish Congress, the Kiwanis Club, and the League of Women Voters are all considered voluntary associations. People of higher socioeconomic status are more likely to belong to and participate actively in such organizations. Reflecting the occupational patterns of the larger society, voluntary associations in the United States are largely segregated by gender. (127)

Technology's Impact on the Workplace: Computer-generated automation has completely transformed the nature of manufacturing and the service sector of the economy. Increasingly, the workforce is turning into telecommuters in many industrial countries. Telecommuters are employees of business firms or government agencies who work full-time at home rather than in an outside office, and who are linked to their supervisors and colleagues through computer terminals, phone lines, and fax machines. (128)

The State of the Union: Labor unions consist of organized workers sharing either the same skill or the same employer. In 1945, unions represented 39 percent of workers in the private sector of the U.S. economy; in 2001, they represented only 14 percent. There are several arguments about the reasons for this decline: changes in industry dominance (manufacturing replaced by service industries); growth of part-time jobs; changes in the legal system; globalization; changes in employer-employee relations; and union rigidity and bureaucratization. Perhaps as a result of all these factors, unions have changed in structure and power. For workers today confidence in unions is low. (129)

KEY TERMS

Briefly define or identify the following terms in the spaces provided below. The definitions of most of these terms can be found later in this chapter of the study guide.

McDonaldization	Formal organization
Group	Bureaucracy
Primary group	Ideal type
Secondary group	Alienation
In-group	Trained incapacity
Out-group	Goal displacement
Reference group	Peter principle
Small group	Bureaucratization

Dyad	Iron law of oligarchy
Triad	Classical theory
Coalition	Scientific management approach
Human relations approach	Telecommuters
Voluntary associations	Labor unions

SELF-TEST

MODIFIED TRUE-FALSE QUESTIONS: If the statement below is true, write "true" in the space provided. If the statement is false, briefly correct the error.

1. People who are flying on the same airplane from New York City to London are members of a group.

2. Members of a primary group, such as neighbors, close friends, and especially kinfolk can play a vital role in assisting people with complicated schedules for taking prescription medicines.

3. Each of the following statements implies the existence of reference groups: "Our generation does not have those sexual hang-ups"; "We Christians go to church every week"; and "We have to support our troops in Bosnia."

4. Patrick Kinkade and Michael Katovich used the functionalist perspective to explore the social relationships that developed among urban pizza delivery drivers as they socialized during work while waiting for orders, and after work in bars.

5. Only one reference group can influence an individual at a given time.

6. Charles Horton Cooley is credited as the first sociologist to emphasize the importance of interaction processes within groups.

7. Adding an additional member to a dyad always serves a unifying role.

8. Elements of bureaucracy are found in about one-third of the occupations in an industrial society such as the United States.

9. The five characteristics of bureaucracies that Weber discussed include division of labor, hierarchy of authority, written rules and regulations, dysfunctions, and impersonality.

10. Although division of labor has certainly been beneficial in the performance of many complex bureaucracies, in some cases it can lead to the Peter principle in which workers become so specialized that they develop blind spots and fail to notice obvious problems.

11. Max Weber used the term goal displacement to refer to overzealous conformity to official regulations.

12. Normally, we think of bureaucratization in terms of large organizations. But bureaucratization also takes place within small-group settings.

13. The iron law of oligarchy describes how even a democratic organization will develop into a bureaucracy ruled by a few (the oligarchy).

14. It was not until workers organized unions, forcing management to recognize that they were not objects, that theorists of formal organizations began to revise the classical approach.

15. Informal understandings among workers can redefine official policies of bureaucracy.

MULTIPLE-CHOICE QUESTIONS: In each of the following, select the phrase that best completes the statement.

1. All of the redheaded people in the United States are an example of a (an)
   a. group.
   b. aggregate.
   c. category.
   d. formal organization.

2. Close friends who have known each other since childhood would be an example of a (an)
   a. primary group.
   b. secondary group.
   c. out-group.
   d. formal organization.

3. _______________ groups often emerge in the workplace among those who share special understandings about their occupation.
   a. Primary
   b. Secondary
   c. Out-
   d. Formal

4. The destructive consequences of tensions between in-groups and out-groups are stressed by
   a. functionalists.
   b. conflict theorists.
   c. interactionists.
   d. classical theorists.

5. The purpose of a reference group is to serve as a (an)
   a. normative function by enforcing standards of conduct and belief.
   b. comparison function by serving as a standard against which people can measure themselves and others.
   c. elimination function by dissolving groups that no longer have a social purpose.
   d. both a and b

6. Which of the following statements about small groups is correct?
   a. All small groups are primary groups.
   b. All small groups are secondary groups.
   c. Many small groups differ from primary groups in that they do not necessarily offer the intimate personal relationships characteristic of primary groups.
   d. both b and c

7. In larger groups each person has
   a. less time to speak.
   b. more points of view to absorb.
   c. a more elaborate structure within which to function.
   d. all of the above

8. Which pioneer of sociology first directed researchers to the significance of bureaucratic structure?
   a. Émile Durkheim
   b. Max Weber
   c. Karl Marx
   d. Ferdinand Tönnies

9. The president of the United States need not be a good typist; a surgeon need not be able to fill a cavity. This is because of the bureaucratic characteristic of
   a. division of labor.
   b. impersonality.
   c. employment based on technical qualifications.
   d. written rules and regulations.

10. Steve is the star of the college football team. He takes a history course and fails all of the exams in that course. Nevertheless, the instructor gives Steve an "A" in the course. This would violate which component of bureaucracies?
   a. division of labor
   b. written rules and regulations
   c. employment based on technical qualifications
   d. impersonality

11. Claude is in a major automobile accident and is severely injured. When he is brought by ambulance to the hospital, he is refused admission because he cannot find his health insurance card. This situation would illustrate
   a. the Peter principle.
   b. trained incapacity.
   c. goal displacement.
   d. division of labor.

12. When Sociologist Jennifer Bickman Mendez studied domestic houseworkers, she found that the impersonality and efficiency of the bureaucratic system in which they worked was yet another example of the ____________ of the workplace.
    a. collectivism
    b. individualism
    c. McDonaldization
    d. none of the above

13. Which of the following have expressed particular concern about the longevity of union leaders who are not always responsive to the needs and demands of membership?
    a. functionalists
    b. conflict theorists
    c. interactionists
    d. classical theorists

14. When workers organized unions and forced management to recognize that they were not objects, theorists of formal organizations began to revise the
    a. classical theory.
    b. scientific management approach.
    c. human relations approach.
    d. both a and b

15. What are the social implications of a shift toward the virtual office—the increasing number of telecommuters?
    a. It may pull mothers and fathers back into the home.
    b. It will increase autonomy and job satisfaction for many employees.
    c. It will lead to greater worker privacy and job security.
    d. both a and b

FILL-IN QUESTIONS: Fill in the blank spaces in the sentences below with the correct words. Where two or more words are required, there will be a corresponding number of blank spaces.

1. People who happen to be in the same place at the same time, such as members of a Broadway theatre audience, are a (an) ____________.

2. The theorist who coined the terms and distinguished between primary and secondary groups was ____________ ____________ ____________.

3. When we find ourselves identifying closely with a group, it is probably a _____________ group.

4. William Graham Sumner distinguished between _____________ and _____________.

5. In many cases, people model their behavior after groups to which they do not belong. These groups are called _____________ groups.

6. Georg Simmel noted that a group with two members is called a (an) _____________ and a group with three members is called a (an) _____________, and both of these are examples of a (an) _____________ group.

7. A third member of a group may try to gain control by having the other two members become rivals. This is known as the _____________-_____________-_____________ strategy.

8. Formal organizations have a (an) _____________ form of organization.

9. Max Weber developed a (an) _____________ _____________ of bureaucracy, which reflects the most characteristic aspects of all human organizations.

10. Trained incapacity, goal displacement, and the Peter principle are all examples of bureaucratic _____________.

11. The division of labor in a bureaucracy can sometimes cause workers to become so specialized that they develop blind spots, and they fail to notice obvious problems. This problem is called _____________ _____________.

12. Every person who walks into a fast food restaurant is greeted with a smile and the statement, "May I take your order, please?" This standardized treatment, characteristic of all bureaucracies, is known as _____________.

13. Robert Michels argues that the rank and file of a movement or organization look to leaders for direction, and thereby reinforce the process of rule by a _____________.

14. The iron law of oligarchy was developed by German sociologist _____________ _____________.

15. _____________ are employees of business or government agencies who work full-time or part-time at home rather than in an outside office, and who are linked to their supervisors and colleagues through computer terminals, phone lines, and fax machines.

UNDERSTANDING SOCIAL POLICY: All the following questions are based on material that appears in the social policy section on the State of the Union. Write a brief answer to each question in the space provided below.

1. What is the definition of a labor union?

2. Give six reasons that account for the decline of labor unions, and explain each.

3. What do conflict theorists and functionalist theorists have in common in the discussion of labor unions?

4. Describe the Right to Work law. How many states have this law, and how does it affect labor unions?

DEFINITIONS OF KEY TERMS

McDonaldization: The process by which the principles of the fast-food restaurant industry have come to dominate certain sectors of society. (116)

Group: Any number of people with similar norms, values, and expectations who regularly and consciously interact. (117)

Primary group: A small group characterized by intimate, face-to-face association and cooperation. (117)

Secondary group: A formal, impersonal group in which there is little social intimacy or mutual understanding. (118)

In-group: Any group or category to which people feel they belong. (118)

Out-group: A group or category to which people feel they do not belong. (119)

Reference group: Any group that individuals use as a standard in evaluating themselves and their own behavior. (119)

Small group: A group small enough for all members to interact simultaneously; that is, to talk with one another or at least be acquainted. (120)

Dyad: A two-member group. (121)

Triad: A three-member group. (121)

Coalition: A temporary or permanent alliance geared toward a common goal. (121)

Formal organization: A special-purpose group designed and structured in the interests of maximum efficiency. (121)

Bureaucracy: A component of formal organizations in which rules and hierarchical ranking are used to achieve efficiency. (122)

Ideal type: A construct or model that serves as a standard for evaluating specific cases. (123)

Alienation: A condition of estrangement or association from the surrounding society. (123)

Trained incapacity: The tendency of workers in a bureaucracy to become so specialized that they develop blind spots, and cannot notice obvious problems. (123)

Goal displacement: Overzealous conformity to official regulations within a bureaucracy. (124)

Peter principle: Any group that individuals use as a standard in evaluating themselves and their own behavior. (125)

Bureaucratization: The process by which a group, organization, or social movement becomes increasingly bureaucratic. (126)

Iron law of oligarchy: A principle of organizational life under which even democratic organizations will become bureaucracies ruled by a few individuals. (126)

Classical theory: An approach to the study of formal organizations that views workers as being motivated almost entirely by economic rewards. (126)

Scientific management approach: Another name for the classical theory of formal organizations. (126)

Human relations approach: An approach to the study of formal organizations that emphasizes the role of people, communication, and participation within a bureaucracy and tends to focus on the informal structure of the organization. (127)

Voluntary associations: Organizations established on the basis of common interest, whose members volunteer or even pay to participate. (127)

Telecommuters: Employees of business firms or government agencies who work full-time or part-time at home rather than in an outside office, and who are linked to their supervisors and colleagues through computer terminals, phone lines, and fax machines. (128)

Labor unions: Labor unions consist of organized workers sharing either the same skill or the same employer. (129)

ANSWERS TO SELF-TEST

Modified True-False Questions

1. People who are flying on the same airplane happen to be in the same place at the same time and are an aggregate. (117)
2. True (117)
3. Each of the phrases implies the existence of in-groups and out-groups—groups to which we feel that we belong or do not belong. (118)
4. Kinkade and Katovich use interactionism in the study of pizza delivery employees. (118)
5. It's not uncommon for two or more reference groups to influence us at the same time. (120)
6. Georg Simmel was the first sociologist to emphasize the importance of interaction processes within groups. (121)
7. Adding an additional person to a dyad may serve a unifying role, a mediating role, or may lead to a divide-and-rule strategy. (121)
8. Elements of bureaucracy enter into almost every occupation in an industrial society. (122)
9. Dysfunctions are not one of the five characteristics of bureaucracy discussed by Max Weber. Employment based on technical qualifications should be added to the list. (123)
10. When workers become so specialized that they develop blind spots and fail to notice obvious problems, it is called trained incapacity. (123)
11. Robert Merton has used the term goal displacement to refer to overzealous conformity to official regulations. (124)
12. True (126)
13. True (126)
14. True (127)
15. True (127)

Multiple-Choice Questions

1. c (117)
2. a (117)
3. b (118)
4. b (119)
5. d (119)
6. c (120)
7. d (120)
8. b (122)
9. a (123)
10. b (124)
11. c (124)
12. c (126)
13. b (126)
14. a (127)
15. d (129)

Fill-In Questions

1. aggregate (117)
2. Charles Horton Cooley (117)
3. primary (117)
4. in-groups; out-groups (118)
5. reference (119)
6. dyad; triad; small (121)
7. divide-and-rule (121)
8. bureaucratic (121)
9. ideal type (123)
10. dysfunctions (123)
11. trained incapacity (123)
12. impersonality (124)
13. few (126)
14. Robert Michels (126)

15. Telecommuters (128)

Understanding Social Policy: Labor Unions

1. Labor unions consist of organized workers sharing either the same skill or the same employer. (129)
2. 1) Changes in the type of industry: Manufacturing jobs, which were the heart of labor unions, have declined, and have been replaced by postindustrial service jobs that typically do not have union representation. 2) Growth of part-time jobs: It was not until 2000 that a part-time employee could enter into a union. 3) Changes in the legal system: government influence has made it increasingly difficult for labor unions to organize and bargain. 4) Globalization: the threat of jobs leaving the country has undercut the ability of union leaders to organize workers at home. 5) Changes in employer-employee relations: employers have become increasingly hostile or rigid in their negotiations with unions, even seeking court actions to block efforts of the union. 6) Union rigidity and bureaucratization: labor unions have been slow to include women, minorities, and immigrants, and have slowly grown more concerned with who leads the organization than with what they are representing. (130)
3. Both Marxists and functionalists would view unions as a logical response to the emergence of impersonal, large-scale, formal, and often alienating organizations. Unions have become increasingly bureaucratized under a self-serving leadership. (130)
4. The Right to Work law states that workers cannot be required to join or pay dues or fees to a union. This is evident in 20 states and displays an anti-union attitude of the citizens. (131)

CHAPTER 7

THE MASS MEDIA

KEY POINTS

Mass Media: By **mass media** sociologists refer to the print and electronic instruments of communication that carry messages to often widespread audiences. The pervasiveness of the mass media in society is obvious. Few aspects of society are as central as the mass media. Through the media we expand our understanding of people and events beyond what we experience in person. For sociologists, the key question is how the mass media affect our social institutions, and how they influence our social behavior. (137)

The Functionalist View: The most obvious function of the mass media is to entertain. We often think the purpose of media is to occupy our leisure time, but they also serve other important functions. The media enforce social norms, confer status, and keep us informed about our social environment. One dysfunction is that the media may act as a narcotic, desensitizing us to events. (137)

Socialization of Mass Media: The media act as an **agent of socialization**. The media increase social cohesion by presenting a more or less standardized common view of culture through mass communication. The mass media unquestionably play a significant role in providing a collective experience for members of a society. (137)

Enforcer of Social Norms: The mass media reaffirm proper behavior by showing what happens to people who act in a way that violates societal expectations. (138)

Conferral of Status: The mass media can also confer status on people, organizations, and public issues by singling out one from thousands of other similarly placed issues or people as significant. The decision-makers within the media organizations generally define the "facts," or determine who to portray to the audience. The collection and distribution of information concerning events in the social environment is the **surveillance function** of the media. (139)

Dysfunctional Media—The Narcotizing Effect: A dysfunction is an element or process of society that may disrupt a social system or lead to a decrease in stability. Some refer to the media as having a **narcotizing dysfunction**. A narcotizing dysfunction refers to the phenomenon where by the media provide such massive amounts of information that the audience becomes numb and generally fails to act on the information they receive regardless of how compelling the issue. (139)

Conflict View: Conflict theorists emphasize that the media reflect and even exacerbate many of the divisions of our society and world, including those based on gender, race, ethnicity, and social class. Within the mass media, a relatively small number of people control what material eventually reaches the audience, a process known as *gatekeeping*. (139)

Gatekeeping: The gatekeepers are overwhelmingly white, male, and prosperous. Conflict theorists argue that the mass media serve to maintain the privileges of certain groups. Moreover, while protecting their own interests, powerful groups may limit the representation of others in the media, such as African Americans, Hispanics, gays and lesbians, people with disabilities, the overweight, and older people. (140)

Feminist View: Feminists continue the argument advanced by conflict theorists that the mass media stereotype and misrepresent social reality. They contend that the media illustrate images of the sexes that are unrealistic, stereotypical, and limit our perceptions of male-female roles. (144)

Interactionist View: Interactionists are especially interested in shared understandings of everyday behavior. They examine the media on the microlevel to see how they shape day-to-day social behavior. The interactionist perspective also helps us to understand more about one important aspect of the entire mass media system—the *audience.* (144)

The Audience: We can look at the audience from both the level of microsociology and macrosociology. At the microlevel we would consider how the audience members interacting among themselves would respond to the media, or in the case of live performances, would interact with the performer or the other members of the audience. At the macrolevel we would examine broader societal consequences of the media, such as early childhood education through programming like *Sesame Street.* (146)

The Segmented Audience: A segmented audience is a portion of all viewers that can be identified and targeted. To some degree, advertising drives the specialization of targeting a segment of an audience. We tend to assume that ***audience behavior*** is universal. But despite the role of opinion leaders (someone who through day-to-day personal contact and communication influences the opinions and decisions of others) members of an audience do not all interpret media in the same way. The audience, then, is not a passive group of people but are active consumers who often are impelled to interact with others about the media event. (146)

The Media Industry: The media industry is getting more and more concentrated with just a handful of multinational corporations dominating the publishing, broadcasting, and film industries. This concentration raises concerns about how innovative and independent the media can continue to be. In some countries, governments own and control the media. The one significant exception to centralization and concentration is the Internet, which allows millions of people to "produce" their own media content. (147)

KEY TERMS

Briefly define or identify the following terms in the spaces provided below. The definitions of these terms can be found later in this chapter of the study guide.

Mass media	Surveillance function
Narcotizing dysfunction	Stereotypes
Gatekeeping	Opinion leader
Dominant ideology	

SELF-TEST

MODIFIED TRUE-FALSE QUESTIONS: If the statement below is true, write "true" in the space provided. If the statement is false, briefly correct the error.

1. Sociologists refer to the print and electronic instruments of communication that carry messages to often widespread audiences as television transmissions.

2. For sociologists, the key question is how the mass media affect our social institutions, and how they influence our social behavior.

3. While the media can serve to reinforce proper behavior, they don't endorse illicit activities, such as drag racing or drug use.

4. In 1997 a federal law required the television networks to provide one free minute for every minute the government bought for a public service announcement with an anti-drug message. The networks have fully complied and continue to support this law.

5. Viewer fatigue begins when the viewer experiences eyestrain and sore fingertips from overuse of the remote control.

6. The mass media constitute a form of big business in which profits are more important than the quality of the product (programming).

7. In many countries the government plays a gatekeeping role. A study for the World Bank found that in 97 countries, only 5 percent of the top five TV stations and only 3 percent of the largest radio stations were government-owned.

8. The Internet is a means of quick dissemination of information or misinformation without going through any significant gatekeeping process.

9. The Internet is totally without restrictions.

10. In 1999 the 26 new prime-time series more evenly portrayed minorities, overweight individuals and disabled individuals, which shows that the broadcasting industry is no longer supportive of biased programming.

11. Media observers believe that the networks will need to integrate the ranks of gatekeepers before they achieve true diversity in programming.

12. Movies produced in the United States account for only 5 percent of the global box office.

13. According to the feminist view, one of the three problems that arise from media coverage is the depiction of male-female relationships emphasizing traditional sex roles and discouraging violence against women.

14. Television literally serves as a babysitter, or a "playmate," for many children and even infants.

15. There are no exceptions to the centralization and concentration of the media.

MULTIPLE-CHOICE QUESTIONS: In each of the following, select the phrase that best completes the statement.

1. Sociologists consider mass media to include
   a. newspapers and magazines.
   b. television and radio.
   c. books and the Internet.
   d. all of the above

2. The most obvious function of the mass media is
   a. to confer status.
   b. to enforce social norms.
   c. to inform us about our social environment.
   d. to entertain.

3. The socialization process of the mass media is not universally regarded. Many people worry about
   a. the effect of using the television as a "babysitter."
   b. the impact of violent programming on viewer behavior.
   c. the unequal ability for all individuals to purchase televisions.
   d. both a and b

4. The narcotizing dysfunction from media coverage of a tragedy can cause the audience
   a. to become numb.
   b. to become desensitized to the suffering.
   c. to conclude that a solution to the crisis has been found.
   d. all of the above

5. In 1997, when networks made an agreement with the government to drop free minutes in exchange for embedding aggressive anti-drug messages in their programs, many thought it was a slippery slope that could
   a. allow an entertainer to quickly slide out of the limelight.
   b. open the way for government to plant messages in the media on topics such as abortion or gun control.
   c. cause the distribution of information related to the social environment.
   d. cause a crash in the stock market.

6. An example of television creating false images or stereotypes of subordinate groups that become accepted as accurate portrayals of reality is
   a. an all-White cast in an urban-based show situated in an ethnically diverse city.
   b. Blacks being repeatedly portrayed and featured in crime-based dramas.
   c. Latinos rarely being present in any television program.
   d. all of the above

7. Comedian Paul Rodriquez once observed that the most prominent Hispanic actor represented on television is
   a. Ricky Ricardo.
   b. Martin Sheen.
   c. the Taco Bell chihuahua dog.
   d. Bill Cosby.

8. Why should it matter that minority groups aren't visible on network television, if they are well represented on cable networks like BET, UPN, and Univision?
   a. Because everyone has the right to be a "star."
   b. According to the equal rights amendment of 1920, all races and nationalities must be equally represented on television.
   c. A societal backlash may occur because minorities feel slighted by under representation.
   d. Whites as well as minorities see a distorted picture of their society every time they turn on network TV.

9. Which perspective contends that the mass media stereotype and misrepresent social reality influencing the way we view men and women?
   a. the functionalist perspective
   b. the conflict perspective
   c. the interactionist perspective
   d. the feminist perspective

10. Which perspective examines the media on a microlevel to see how they shape day-to-day social behavior?
    a. the functionalist perspective
    b. the conflict perspective
    c. the interactionist perspective
    d. the feminist perspective

11. The one thing all media need to exist is
    a. cameras.
    b. fiber optic lines.
    c. laser dish transmission.
    d. an audience.

12. There are concerns about whether the public interest is being served by the growing concentration of media. One major concern is
    a. propaganda in radio transmissions.
    b. that innovation and independence will decline.
    c. Internet fraud and crime.
    d. none of the above

13. In the United States the gatekeeping process is
    a. in the hands of private individuals who desire to maximize profits.
    b. with political leaders who desire to maintain control of the government.
    c. with church leaders who desire to maintain control of the government.
    d. none of the above

14. Before 1999 the country of Bhutan strictly controlled the influence of the mass media on their society. What effects have been observed since 1999?
    a. Sitcoms and action films have overshadowed the traditional spoken stories that transmit values.
    b. Young girls dance the latest steps shown on MTV while young boys sport homemade World Wrestling Federation belts.
    c. Language that was previously rarely heard has now entered everyday speech.
    d. all of the above

15. The key to creating a truly global network that reaches directly into workplaces, schools, and homes is
    a. cable networks.
    b. XFM radio broadcasting.
    c. distribution of major print media.
    d. the Internet.

FILL-IN QUESTIONS: Fill in the blank spaces in the sentences below with the correct words. Where two or more words are required, there will be a corresponding number of blank spaces.

1. For sociologists, the key question is how the mass media affect our ________________ ________________ and how they influence our ________________ ________________.

2. In 1997, a federal law required television networks to provide one free minute for every minute the government bought for a public service announcement with a ________________ announcement.

3. The ________________ generally define what are "facts" for the audience, using a definition that reflects the values and orientation of the decision makers within media organizations.

4. Paul Lazarsfeld and Robert Merton created the term _______________ _______________ to refer to the phenomenon whereby the media provide such massive amounts of information that the audience becomes numb, and generally fails to act on the information, regardless of how compelling the issue.

5. The _______________ perspective contends that television distorts the political process.

6. The content of media may create false images or _______________ of subordinate groups.

7. We risk being _______________ if we overstress U.S. dominance and assume other nations do not play a role in media cultural exports.

8. _______________ examine the media on the microlevel to see how they shape day-to-day social behavior.

9. _______________ _______________ goes beyond films, books, magazines, and TV programs. It also applies to what ideas and facts get transmitted.

10. The same people, by and large, who experience poor health and have few job opportunities also have been left off the _______________ _______________.

11. The _______________ perspective helps us to understand more about one important aspect of the entire mass media system, the _______________.

12. We can point to a handful of _______________ _______________ that dominate the publishing, broadcasting, and film industries.

13. Today, _______________ _______________ is no longer a barrier, and instant messaging is possible across the world.

14. _______________ _______________ of television programming show that media have gradually become more violent, even programs targeted to children.

15. Both _______________ and _______________ theorists are troubled that the victims depicted in violent imagery are often those who are given less respect in real life: women, children, the poor, racial minorities, citizens of foreign countries and even the physically disabled.

UNDERSTANDING SOCIAL POLICY: All the following questions are based on material that appears in the social policy section on Media Violence. Write a brief answer to each question in the space provided below.

1. The controversy surrounding violence and the media raises basic questions about the function of the media. How do conflict and feminist theorists interpret the violence in the media?

2. How do interactionists interpret the violence in the media?

3. How have policy makers responded to the issue of violence in the media?

DEFINITION OF KEY TERMS

Mass media: The print and electronic instruments of communication that carry messages to often widespread audiences. (137)

Surveillance function: The collection and distribution of information concerning events in the social environment. (139)

Narcotizing dysfunction: A narcotizing dysfunction refers to the phenomenon whereby the media provide such massive amounts of information that the audience becomes numb and generally fails to act on the information they receive regardless of how compelling the issue. (139)

Gatekeeping: The process by which a relatively small number of people control what material eventually reaches the audience. (140)

Dominant ideology: The set of cultural beliefs and practices that help to maintain powerful social, economic, and political interests. (141)

Stereotypes: Unreliable generalizations about all members of a group that do not recognize individual differences within the group. (142)

Opinion leader: Someone who, through day-to-day personal contact and communication, influences the opinions and decisions of others. (146)

ANSWERS TO SELF-TEST

Modified True-False Questions

1. Sociologists refer to the print and electronic instruments of communication that carry messages to often widespread audiences as mass media. (137)
2. True (137)
3. While the media can serve to reinforce proper behavior, they may also endorse illicit activity, such as drag racing down city streets and drug use. (138)
4. In 1997 a federal law required the television networks to provide one free minute for every minute the government bought for a public service announcement with an anti-drug message. However, the networks subsequently made an agreement with the government to drop the free minutes in exchange for embedding aggressive anti-drug messages in their programs, such as *ER*, *The Practice*, and *Sabrina the Teenage Witch*. (138)
5. Viewer fatigue begins when media coverage of a tragedy, such as a natural disaster or family crisis, is prolonged. (139)
6. True (140)
7. The study for the World Bank found that in 97 countries, 60 percent of the top five TV stations and 72 percent of the largest radio stations were government-owned. (140)
8. True (141)
9. The Internet is not totally without restrictions. Laws in many nations try to regulate content on such issues as gambling, pornography, and even political views, and popular Internet service providers will terminate accounts for offensive behavior. (141)
10. In late spring 1999, in all 26 new primetime series, all leading characters, as well as the vast majority of the supporting casts, were White. (142)
11. True (143)
12. Movies produced in the United States account for 65 percent of the global box office. (143)
13. According to the feminist view, one of the three problems that arises from media coverage is the depiction of male-female relationships, which emphasizes traditional sex roles and *normalizes* violence against women. (144)
14. True (145)
15. There is one exception to the centralization and concentration of the media—the Internet. (148)

Multiple-Choice Questions

1.	d (137)	6.	d (142)	11.	d (146)
2.	d (137)	7.	c (142)	12.	b (147)
3.	d (138)	8.	d (142)	13.	d (148)
4.	d (139)	9.	d (144)	14.	d (148)
5.	b (139)	10.	c (144)	15.	d (149)

Fill-In Questions

1.	social institutions; social behavior (137)	6.	stereotypes (142)
2.	anti-drug (138)	7.	ethnocentric (144)
3.	media (139)	8.	Interactionists (144)
4.	narcotizing dysfunction (139)	9.	Cultural domination (144)
5.	Conflict (142)	10.	information highway (145)

11. interactionist; audience (145)
12. multinational corporations (147)
13. physical distance (148)
14. Content analyses (150)
15. conflict; feminist (151)

UNDERSTANDING SOCIAL POLICY: Media Violence

1. Media violence raises questions of the function of media. If the function is to entertain, socialize, and enforce social norms, how can violence be a part of that message? Conflict and feminist theorists are troubled that the victims depicted in violent imagery are often those who are given less respect in real life: women, children, the poor, racial minorities, citizens of foreign countries, and even the physically disabled. (151)
2. Interactionists are especially interested in finding out if violence in the media may later become a script for real-life behavior. Aggression is a product of socialization and people may model themselves after the violent behavior they see. (151)
3. Policy makers have responded to the links between violence depicted in the media and real-life aggression on two levels. (1) In public statements politicians are quick to call for more family-oriented, less violent content. However, on the (2) legislative level, policy makers are reluctant to engage in what could be regarded as censorship. (152)

CHAPTER

8 DEVIANCE AND SOCIAL CONTROL

Social Control

Deviance

Crime

Social Policy and Social Control: The Death Penalty in the United States and Worldwide

BOXES

***RESEARCH IN ACTION**: Defining Deviancy Down: From Professional Wrestling to the Backyards*

***SOCIAL INEQUALITY**: Discretionary Justice*

***TAKING SOCIOLOGY TO WORK**: Tiffany Zapata-Mancilla, Victim Witness Specialist, Code County State Attorney's Office*

KEY POINTS

Social Control: The term **social control** refers to the techniques and strategies for preventing deviant human behavior in any society. Social control occurs on all levels of society—in the family, in peer groups, and in bureaucratic organizations. Most of us respect and accept basic social norms and assume that others will do the same. If we fail to act "properly," we may face punishment through informal **sanctions**, such as fear and ridicule, or formal sanctions, such as jail sentences or fines. (157)

Conformity and Obedience: Stanley Milgram made a useful distinction between two important levels of social control. He defined **conformity** as going along with one's peers—individuals of a person's own status, who have no special right to direct that person's behavior. By contrast, **obedience** is defined as compliance with higher authorities in a hierarchical structure. (158)

Informal and Formal Social Control: **Informal social control** is social control carried out by people casually through such means as smiles, laughter, and ridicule. **Formal social control** is carried out by authorized agents, such as police officers, physicians, school administrators, employers, military officers, and managers of movie theaters. It can serve as a last resort when socialization and informal sanctions do not bring about desired behavior. (160)

Law and Society: Some norms are so important to a society that they are formalized into **laws** controlling people's behavior. Law is governmental social control. Sociologists have become increasingly interested in the creation of laws as a social process. In their view, law is not merely a static body of rules handed down from generation to generation. Rather it reflects continually changing standards of what is right and wrong, of how violations are to be determined, and of what sanctions are to be applied. (161)

Deviance: For sociologists, **deviance** is behavior that violates the standards of conduct or expectations of a group or society. Deviance involves the violations of group norms that may or may not be formalized into law. It is a comprehensive concept that includes not only criminal behavior but also many actions not subject to prosecution. Deviance can be understood only within its social context. (162)

Deviance and Social Stigma: While deviance can include relatively minor day-to-day decisions about our personal behavior, in some cases it can become part of a person's identity. This process is called **stigmatization**. The interactionist Erving Goffman coined the term **stigma** to describe the labels society uses to devalue members of certain social groups. Often people are stigmatized for deviant behaviors they may no longer engage in. Goffman draws a useful distinction between a prestige symbol that draws attention to a positive aspect of one's identity, such as a wedding band or a badge, and a stigma symbol that discredits or debases one's identity, such as a conviction for child molestation. (163)

The Functionalist View: According to functionalists, deviance is a normal part of human existence, with positive (as well as negative) consequences for social stability. Deviance helps to define the limits of proper behavior. As Émile Durkheim observed, the punishments established within a culture (including both formal and informal mechanisms of social control) help to define acceptable behavior and thus contribute to stability. If improper acts were not committed and then sanctioned, people might stretch their standards as to what constitutes appropriate conduct. (168)

Merton's Theory of Deviance: Using a functionalist analysis, Robert Merton adapted Durkheim's notion of anomie to explain why people accept or reject the goals of a society, the socially approved means of fulfilling their aspirations, or both. Merton developed the **anomie theory of deviance**, which posits five basic forms of adaptation. (1) Conformity to social norms, the most common adaptation in Merton's typology, is the opposite of deviance. It involves acceptance of both the overall societal goal and the approved means. (2) The "innovator" accepts the goals of a society but pursues them with means regarded as improper. (3) The "ritualist" has abandoned the goal of material success and becomes compulsively committed to the institutional means. (4) The "retreatist" has basically withdrawn from both the goals and the means of a society, and (5) the "rebel" feels alienated from dominant means and goals, and may seek a dramatically different social order. (168)

Cultural Transmission and Differential Association: Sociologist Edwin Sutherland drew upon the **cultural transmission** school of criminology, which emphasizes that criminal behavior is learned through interactions with others. Sutherland maintained that through interactions with a primary group and significant others, people acquire definitions of behavior that are deemed proper and improper. He used the term **differential association** to describe the process through which exposure to attitudes favorable to criminal acts leads to violation of rules. People are more likely to engage in norm-defying behavior if they are part of a group or subculture that stresses deviant values. (169)

Labeling Theory: Reflecting the contribution of interactionist theorists, **labeling theory** attempts to explain why certain people are perceived as deviants, while others with similar behavior are not. Labeling theory is also called the **societal-reaction approach**, reminding us that it is the response to an act, and not the behavior that determines deviance. An important aspect of labeling theory is the recognition that some people or groups have the power to define labels and apply them to others. The popularity of labeling theory is reflected in the emergence of a related perspective called social constructionism. According to the **social constructionist perspective**, deviance is the product of the culture we live in. Social constructionists focus specifically on the decision-making process that creates the deviant identity. (171)

The Conflict View of Deviance: Why is certain behavior evaluated as deviant while other behavior is not? According to conflict theorists, it is because people with power protect their own interests and define deviance to suit their own needs. Sociologist Richard Quinney and other conflict theorists argue that lawmaking is often an attempt by the powerful to coerce others into their own brand of morality. On the whole, conflict theorists contend that the criminal justice system of the United States treats suspects and offenders differently on the basis of racial, ethnic, and social class backgrounds. (172)

Feminist Perspective: When it comes to crime and to deviance in general, society tends to treat women in a stereotypical fashion. Cultural views and attitudes towards women influence how they are perceived and labeled. The feminist perspective emphasizes that deviance, including crime, tends to flow from economic relationships. (174)

Crime Statistics: Crime statistics are not as accurate as social scientists would like. Reported crime is very high in the United States, and the public continues to regard crime as a major social problem. However, there has been a significant decline in violent crime nationwide in the United States following many years of increases. Sociologists have several ways of measuring crime. Partly because of the deficiencies of official statistics, the National Crime Survey was initiated in 1972. The Bureau of Justice Statistics, in compiling this report, seeks information from law enforcement agencies, but also interviews members of 45,000 households annually, and asks if they have been victims of a specific set of crimes during the preceding year. In general, **victimization surveys** question ordinary people, not police officers, to learn how much crime occurs. (177)

International Crime Rates: During the 1980s and 1990s violent crimes were much more common in the United States than in Western Europe. Yet the incidence of certain other types of crime appears to be higher elsewhere. For example, England, Italy, Australia, and New Zealand all have higher rates of car theft than the United States, while the Czech Republic has a higher burglary rate. (178)

KEY TERMS

Briefly define or identify the following terms in the spaces provided below. The definitions of these terms can be found later in this chapter of the study guide.

Social control	Informal social control
Sanctions	Formal social control

Conformity	Law
Obedience	Control theory
Deviance	Societal-reaction approach
Stigma	Social constructionist perspective
Anomie	Crime
Anomie theory of deviance	Professional criminal
Cultural transmission	Organized crime
Differential association	White-collar crimes
Routine activities theory	Victimless crimes
Labeling theory	Victimization surveys

SELF-TEST

MODIFIED TRUE-FALSE QUESTIONS: If the statement below is true, write “true” in the space provided. If the statement is false, briefly correct the error.

1. Binge drinking is always regarded as deviant behavior.

2. A recruit entering military service will typically obey the habits and language of other recruits, and will conform to the orders of superior officers.

3. An experiment conducted at Smith College found that statements overheard by others influence expressions of opinion on the issue of racism.

4. Viewed from an interactionist perspective, one important aspect of Milgram’s findings concerning obedience to authority is that subjects in follow-up studies were more likely to inflict the supposed shocks as they were moved physically closer to their victims.

5. A 1998 policy statement by the American Academy of Pediatrics that corporal punishment is not effective and can be harmful is supported by the majority of child development specialists and pediatricians in the United States.

6. In the view of sociologists, law is a static body of rules handed down from generation to generation.

7. Conflict theory suggests that our connection to members of society leads us to systematically conform to society's norms.

8. According to functionalists, deviance has only negative consequences for social stability.

9. Robert Merton made a key contribution to sociological understanding of deviance by pointing out that deviants share a great deal with conforming people.

10. Sociologist Edwin Sutherland popularized labeling theory.

11. Researchers have found that discretionary differences in the way social control is exercised puts deprived African Americans and Hispanics at a disadvantage in the justice system—both as juveniles and as adults.

12. Organized crime dominates the world of illegal business, just as large corporations dominate the conventional business world.

13. Conviction for a white-collar crime has serious implications for an individual's reputation and career aspirations.

14. The conflict perspective argues that the criminal justice system largely disregards the white-collar crimes of the affluent, while focusing on index crimes often committed by the poor.

15. Sociologists agree that the high rates of violent crimes in the United States are the result of the emphasis our society places on individual economic achievement.

MULTIPLE-CHOICE QUESTIONS: In each of the following, select the phrase that best completes the statement.

1. If we fail to respect and obey social norms, we may face punishment through informal or formal
   a. techniques of neutralization.
   b. deviance.
   c. cultural transmission.
   d. sanctions.

2. Which sociological perspective emphasizes that societies literally could not function if massive numbers of people defied standards of appropriate conduct?
   a. the functionalist perspective
   b. the conflict perspective
   c. the interactionist perspective
   d. labeling theory

3. A useful distinction between conformity and obedience was made by social psychologist
   a. Richard Quinney.
   b. Émile Durkheim.
   c. Edwin Sutherland.
   d. Stanley Milgram.

4. Which of the following suggested that the punishments established within a culture help to define acceptable behavior, and thus contribute to stability?
   a. William Chambliss
   b. Émile Durkheim
   c. Richard Quinney
   d. Stanley Milgram

5. The most common adaptation in the anomie theory of deviance is
   a. conformity.
   b. innovation.
   c. ritualism.
   d. rebellion.

6. A burglar who wants to live in the suburbs along with lawyers and stockbrokers will pursue material success by violating the law. In Robert Merton's terms, the burglar is a (an)
   a. ritualist.
   b. retreatist.
   c. rebel.
   d. innovator.

7. In Merton's terms, a person who has abandoned the goal of material success and become compulsively committed to institutional means is a (an)
   a. ritualist.
   b. retreatist.
   c. rebel.
   d. innovator.

8. Which of the following conducted observation research on two groups of high school males (the Saints and the Roughnecks), and concluded that social class played an important role in the varying fortunes of the two groups?
   a. Richard Quinney
   b. Edwin Sutherland
   c. Émile Durkheim
   d. William Chambliss

9. An important aspect of labeling theory is the recognition that some people or groups have the power to define labels and apply them to others. This view recalls the emphasis placed on the social significance of power by the
   a. functionalist perspective.
   b. conflict perspective.
   c. interactionist perspective.
   d. anomie theory of deviance.

10. Which of the following is a leading exponent of the view that the criminal justice system serves the interests of the powerful?
    a. Richard Quinney
    b. Edwin Sutherland
    c. Stanley Milgram
    d. William Chambliss

11. _____________ theorists view standards of deviant behavior as merely reflecting cultural norms; whereas _____________ and _____________ theorists point out that the most powerful groups in a society can shape laws and standards and determine who is (or is not) prosecuted as a criminal.
    a. Conflict; functionalist; labeling
    b. Labeling; conflict; functionalist
    c. Functionalist; conflict; labeling
    d. Conflict; labeling; functionalist

12. Which of the following offered pioneering insights regarding professional criminals by publishing an annotated account written by a professional thief?
    a. Robert Merton
    b. Émile Durkheim
    c. Howard S. Becker
    d. Edwin Sutherland

13. Which of the following is considered a white-collar crime?
    a. consumer fraud
    b. bribery
    c. income tax evasion
    d. all of the above

14. Gambling, public drunkenness, prostitution, and smoking marijuana are
    a. white-collar crimes.
    b. violent crimes against people.
    c. victimless crimes.
    d. organized crime.

15. Which one of the following crime rates was higher in the United States than in Europe during the 1980s and 1990s?
    a. murder
    b. rape
    c. robbery
    d. all of the above

FILL-IN QUESTIONS: Fill in the blank spaces in the sentences below with the correct words. Where two or more words are required, there will be a corresponding number of blank spaces.

1. ______________ theorists are concerned that "successful functioning" of a society will consistently benefit the powerful and work to the disadvantage of other groups.

2. In the United States, one common and controversial example of ______________ social control is parental use of corporal punishment.

3. ______________ social control is carried out by authorized agents, such as police officers, judges, administrators, employers, military officers, and managers of movie theaters.

4. Some norms are considered so important by a society that they are formalized into ______________ controlling people's behavior.

5. It is important to underscore the fact that ______________ is the primary source of conformity and obedience, including obedience to law.

6. ______________ involves the violation of group norms that may or may not be formalized into law.

7. In general, sociologists reject any emphasis on ______________ roots of crime and deviance.

8. ______________ is a state of normlessness that typically occurs during a period of profound social change and disorder, such as a time of economic collapse.

9. Sociologist ______________ ______________ advanced the argument than an individual undergoes the same basic socialization process whether learning conforming or deviant acts.

10. ______________ ______________ ______________, a recent interactionist explanation of deviance, considers that for the requisite conditions for a crime or deviant act to occur, there must be at the same time and in the same place, a perpetrator, a victim, and/or an object of property.

11. ______________ theorists argue that lawmaking is often an attempt by the powerful to coerce others into their own brand of morality.

12. ______________ represents some type of deviation from formal social norms for which some governmental authority applies formal penalties.

13. Daniel Bell used the term ______________ ______________ to describe the process during which leadership of organized crime was transferred from Irish Americans to Jewish Americans and later to Italian Americans and others.

14. Organizations such as Mothers Against Drunk Driving (MADD) and Students Against Drunk Driving (SADD) have had success in recent years in shifting public attitudes toward drunkenness, so that it is no longer being viewed as a "______________ crime."

15. According to the U.N. Human Rights Commission, only ______________ nations permit the execution of defendants who committed their crimes before the age of 18.

UNDERSTANDING SOCIAL POLICY: All the following questions are based on material that appears in the social policy section on The Death Penalty in the United States and Worldwide. Write a brief answer to each question in the space provided below.

1. How does the use of the death penalty in the United States compare to its use in other nations?

2. Discuss the major provision of each of the following United States Supreme Court decisions: *Furman v. Georgia* in 1972, and *Gregg v. Georgia* in 1976.

3. What are the major points that are cited by functionalists in their analysis of the death penalty?

4. What are the major points that are cited by conflict theorists in their analysis of the death penalty?

DEFINITIONS OF KEY TERMS

Social control: The techniques and strategies for preventing deviant human behavior in any society. (157)

Sanctions: Penalties and rewards for conduct concerning a social norm. (158)

Conformity: Going along with one's peers, individuals of a person's own status, who have no special right to direct that person's behavior. (158)

Obedience: Compliance with higher authorities in a hierarchical structure. (158)

Informal social control: Social control carried out by people casually through such means as laughter, smiles, and ridicule. (160)

Formal social control: Social control carried out by authorized agents, such as police officers, judges, school administrators, and employers. (160)

Law: Governmental social control. (161)

Control theory: A view of conformity and deviance that suggests that our connection to members of society leads us to systematically conform to society's norms. (161)

Deviance: Behavior that violates the standards of conduct or expectations of a group or society. (162)

Stigma: A label used to devalue members of deviant social groups. (166)

Anomie: Durkheim's term for the loss of direction felt in a society when social control of individual behavior has become ineffective. (168)

Anomie theory of deviance: Robert Merton's theory that explains deviance as an adaptation either of socially prescribed goals or of the norms governing their attainment, or both. (168)

Cultural transmission: A school of criminology that argues that criminal behavior is learned through social interactions. (169)

Differential association: A theory of deviance proposed by Edwin Sutherland that holds that violation of rules results from exposure to attitudes favorable to criminal acts. (170)

Routine activities theory: The notion that criminal victimization increases when there is a convergence of motivated offenders and suitable targets. (170)

Labeling theory: An approach to deviance popularized by Howard S. Becker that attempts to explain why certain people are viewed as deviants while others engaging in the same behavior are not. (171)

Societal-reaction approach: Another name for labeling theory. (171)

Social constructionist perspective: An approach to deviance that emphasizes the role of culture in the creation of the deviant identity. (172)

Crime: A violation of criminal law for which some governmental authority applies formal penalties. (175)

Professional criminal: A person who pursues crime as a day-to-day occupation, developing skilled techniques and enjoying a certain degree of status among other criminals. (175)

Organized crime: The work of a group that regulates relations between various criminal enterprises involved in the smuggling and sale of drugs, prostitution, gambling, and other illegal activities. (175)

White-collar crimes: Crimes committed by affluent individuals or corporations in the course of their daily business activities. (176)

Victimless crimes: A term used by sociologists to describe the willing exchange among adults of widely desired, but illegal, goods and services. (176)

Victimization survey: Questionnaires or interviews used to determine whether people have been victims of crime. (177)

ANSWERS TO SELF-TEST

Modified True-False Questions

1. On the one hand, binge drinking can be regarded as deviant, violating the standards of conduct expected of those in an academic setting. The other side of this potentially self-destructive behavior is that binge drinking represents conformity to the peer culture. (158)
2. A recruit entering military service will typically *conform* to the habits and language of other recruits, and will *obey* the orders of superior officers. (158)
3. True (159)
4. Viewed from an interactionist perspective, one important aspect of Milgram's findings is that subjects in follow-up studies were less likely to inflict the supposed shocks as they were moved physically closer to their victims. (160)
5. Despite a 1998 policy statement by the American Academy of Pediatrics that corporal punishment is not effective and can be harmful, 59 percent of pediatricians support the use of corporal punishment. (160)
6. In the view of sociologists, law is not merely a static body of rules handed down from generation to generation. Rather, it reflects continually changing standards of what is right and wrong, of how violations are to be determined, and of what sanctions are to be applied. (161)
7. Control theory suggests that our connection to members of society leads us to systematically conform to society's norms. (161)
8. According to functionalists, deviance is a normal part of human existence with positive (as well as negative) consequences for social stability. (168)
9. True (169)
10. Sociologist Howard S. Becker popularized labeling theory. (171)
11. True (173)
12. True (175)
13. Conviction for white-collar crimes does not generally harm a person's reputation and career aspirations nearly as much as conviction for an index crime would. (176)
14. True (176)
15. Sociologists suggest that the United States: places a greater emphasis on individual economic achievement than do other societies; tolerates, if not condones, many forms of violence; has sharp disparities between poor and affluent citizens; has significant unemployment; and has substantial alcohol and drug abuse, all of which produce a climate conducive to crime. (178)

Multiple-Choice Questions

1.	d (158)	5.	a (169)	9.	b (171)	13.	d (176)
2.	a (158)	6.	d (162)	10.	a (172)	14.	c (177)
3.	d (158)	7.	a (169)	11.	c (172)	15.	d (178)
4.	b (168)	8.	d (171)	12.	d (176)		

Fill-In Questions

1. Conflict (158)
2. informal (160)
3. Formal (160)
4. laws (161)
5. socialization (161)
6. Deviance (162)
7. genetic (167)
8. Anomie (168)

9. Edwin Sutherland (169)
10. Routine activities theory (170)
11. Conflict (172)
12. Crime (175)
13. ethnic succession (175)
14. victimless (177)
15. five (179)

Understanding Social Policy: The Death Penalty in the United States and Worldwide

1. In 1997 the UN Human Rights Commission called for a moratorium on capital punishment. In particular, It noted that only five nations permit the execution of defendants who committed their crimes under the age of 18—the United States, Iran, Pakistan, Saudi Arabia, and Yemen. The countries executing the most people were (in order): China, Ukraine, Russia, Turkmenistan, Iran, Saudi Arabia, and the United States. (179)
2. In a landmark 5-4 decision in 1972, *Furman v. Georgia*, the Court held that state death penalty laws, as were then administered, were unconstitutional because the states allowed too much discretion to judges and juries in applying the death sentence. In *Gregg v. Georgia* in 1976, the Court specifically ruled that capital punishment, if administered under the Court's guidelines, was constitutional. (179)
3. Viewed from the functionalist perspective of Émile Durkheim, sanctioning of deviant acts helps to reinforce the standards of proper behavior within society. While the functionalist perspective notes the purpose behind the death penalty, there are also dysfunctions. Many citizens are concerned that the alternative to execution—life sentences in prison—is unnecessarily expensive. (180)
4. The conflict perspective emphasizes the persistence of social inequality in society today. The American Bar Association (1997) has repeatedly expressed concern about the typically limited defense most defendants facing the death penalty receive. Numerous studies show that defendants are more likely to be sentenced to death if their victims were White rather than Black. There is also some evidence that Black defendants, who constitute 42 percent of all death row inmates, are more likely to face execution as compared to Whites in the same legal circumstances. (180)

CHAPTER 9

STRATIFICATION IN THE UNITED STATES AND WORLDWIDE

KEY POINTS

Stratification and Social Inequality: The term **social inequality** describes a condition in which members of a society have different amounts of wealth, prestige, or power. Some degree of social inequality characterizes every society. When a system of social inequality is based on a hierarchy of groups, sociologists refer to it as **stratification**: a structured ranking of entire groups of people that perpetuates unequal economic rewards and power in a society. Ascribed status is a social position "assigned" to a person without regard for that person's unique characteristics or talents. By contrast, achieved status is a social position attained by a person largely through his or her own effort. (187)

The Class System of the United States: Sociologist Daniel Rossides has conceptualized the class system of the United States using a five-class model. Rossides categorized about 1 to 2 percent of the people in the United States as upper class. By contrast, the lower class, consisting of approximately 20 to 25 percent of the population, disproportionately consists of Blacks, Hispanics, single mothers with dependent children, and people who cannot find regular work or must make do with low-paying jobs. Sandwiched between the upper and lower classes in Rossides's model are the upper-middle class, the lower-middle class, and the working class. (189)

Karl Marx's View of Class Differentiation: Karl Marx viewed **class differentiation** as the crucial determinant of social, economic, and political inequality. Marx focused on the two classes that began to emerge as the estate system declined—the **bourgeoisie** and the **proletariat**. The bourgeoisie, or capitalist class, owns the means of production, such as factories and machinery, while the proletariat is the working class. According to Marx, exploitation of the proletariat will inevitably lead to the destruction of the capitalist system. Ultimately, the proletariat will overthrow the rule of the bourgeoisie and the government (which Marx saw as representing the interests of capitalists). (192)

Max Weber's View of Stratification: Unlike Karl Marx, Max Weber insisted that no single characteristic (such as class) totally defines a person's position within the stratification system. He identified three analytically distinct components of stratification: **class, status, and power**. A person's position in a stratification system reflects some combination of his or her class, status, and power. At the same time, these three dimensions of stratification may operate somewhat independently in determining a person's position. (193)

The Functionalist View of Stratification: In the view of Kingsley Davis and Wilbert Moore, society must distribute its members among a variety of social positions. Davis and Moore argue that stratification is universal and that social inequality is necessary so that people will be motivated to fill functionally important positions. However, critics note that even if stratification is inevitable, the functionalist explanation for differential rewards does not explain the wide disparity between the rich and the poor. (194)

The Conflict View of Stratification: Contemporary conflict theorists believe that human beings are prone to conflict over such scarce resources as wealth, status, and power. However, where Marx focused primarily on class conflict, more recent theorists have extended this analysis to include conflicts based on gender, race, age, and other dimensions. Conflict theorists see stratification as a major source of societal tension and conflict. They do not agree that stratification is functional for a society or that it serves as a source of stability. Rather, conflict sociologists argue that stratification will inevitably lead to instability and to social change. (195)

Lenski's View of Stratification: Gerhard Lenski, Jr., described how economic systems change as their level of technology becomes more complex, beginning with hunting and gathering and culminating eventually with industrial society. As a society advances in technology, it becomes capable of producing a considerable surplus of goods. The emergence of surplus resources greatly expands the possibilities for inequality in status, influence, and power, and allows a well-defined, rigid class system to develop. (196)

Wealth and Income in the United States: By all measures, income in the United States is unevenly distributed. In 2000, members of the richest fifth (or top 20 percent) of the nation's population earned $141,621, and accounted for 50 percent of the nation's income. The income gap between the richest and the poorest groups in the United States is widening. Wealth in the United States is much more unevenly distributed than income. In 1997 the richest fifth of the population held 85 percent of the nation's wealth. (198)

Poverty in the United States: Approximately one out of every nine people in the United States lives below the poverty line established by the federal government. Included among the poor of the United States are women and children living in single-parent families with their mothers. In 2001, 41 percent of poor people in the United States were living in central cities. According to many observers, the plight of the urban poor is growing worse because of the devastating interplay of inadequate education and limited employment prospects. William Julius Wilson and other social scientists have used the term **underclass** to describe long-term poor people who lack training and skills. (199)

Social Mobility in the United States: The belief in upward **mobility** is an important aspect of our society. Occupational mobility (which can be **intergenerational** or **intragenerational**) has been common among males. However, occupational mobility among African Americans remains sharply limited by racial discrimination. The impact of education on mobility has diminished somewhat in the last decade. Gender, like race, is an important factor in one's mobility. In contrast to men, women have a rather large range of clerical occupations open to them. But the modest salary ranges and limited prospects for advancement in many of these positions means that there is not much possibility of upward mobility. (204)

Colonialism and Neocolonialism: Colonialism is the maintenance of political, social, economic, and cultural domination over a people by a foreign power for an extended period of time. In simple terms, it is rule by outsiders. By the 1980s, colonialism had largely disappeared—most of the world's nations that were colonies before World War I had achieved political independence and established their own governments by this time. However, their dependence on more industrialized nations, including their former colonial masters, for managerial and technical expertise, investment capital, and manufactured goods, kept former colonies in a subservient position. Such continuing dependence and foreign domination constitute neocolonialism. (208)

World Systems Analysis and Dependency Theory: Drawing on the conflict perspective, sociologist Immanuel Wallerstein views the global economic system as divided between nations who control wealth and those from whom capital is taken. Wallerstein has advanced a world systems analysis to describe the unequal economic and political relationships in which certain industrialized nations (among them, the United States, Japan, and Germany) and their corporations dominate the **core** of the system. Wallerstein suggests that the poor developing countries of Asia, Africa, and Latin America are on the **periphery** of the world economic system. Core nations and their corporations control and exploit the developing nations' economies, much as the old colonial empires ruled their colonies. (208)

Globalization: **Globalization** is the worldwide integration of government policies, cultures, social movements, and financial markets through trade and the exchange of ideas. Embedded in the concept of globalization is the notion of the cultural domination of periphery nations by the core nations. (208)

Multinational Corporations: The term **multinational corporation** refers to commercial organizations that are headquartered in one country but do business throughout the world. Conflict theorists conclude that, on the whole, multinational corporations have a negative social impact on workers in both industrialized and developing nations. Workers in the United States and other core countries are beginning to recognize that their own interests are served by helping to organize workers in developing nations. As long as multinationals can exploit cheap labor abroad, they will be in a strong position to reduce wages and benefits in industrialized countries. (209)

Modernization and Modernization Theory: Contemporary social scientists use the term **modernization** to describe the far-reaching process by which peripheral nations move from traditional or less developed institutions to those characteristic of more developed societies. Many sociologists are quick to note that terms such as modernization, and even development, contain an ethnocentric bias. There is similar criticism of **modernization theory**, a functionalist approach that proposes that modernization and development will gradually improve the lives of people in developing nations. According to this theory, while countries develop at uneven rates, development in peripheral countries will be assisted by the innovations transferred from the industrialized world. (211)

Stratification within Nations—A Comparative Perspective: At the same time that the gap between rich and poor nations is widening, so too is the gap between rich and poor citizens within developing nations. Local elites prosper while industrial and agricultural workers are exploited. Women in developing countries find life especially difficult. (212)

Rethinking Welfare in North America and Europe: In 1996, the Personal Responsibility and Work Opportunity Reconciliation Act ended the long-standing federal guarantee of assistance to every poor family that meets eligibility requirements. It set a lifetime limit of five years of welfare benefits for recipients and required that all able-bodied adults work after two years of benefits (although hardship exceptions are allowed). From a conflict perspective, this backlash against welfare recipients reflects deep fears and hostility toward the nation's urban and predominantly African American and Hispanic underclass. Those who take a conflict perspective also urge policy makers and the general public to look closely at corporate welfare, the tax breaks, direct payments, and grants that the government makes to corporations, rather than focus on the relatively small allowances being given to welfare mothers and their children. (213)

KEY TERMS

Briefly define or identify the following terms in the spaces provided below. The definitions of these terms can be found later in this chapter of the study guide.

Social inequality	Achieved status
Stratification	Slavery
Income	Castes
Wealth	Class system
Ascribed status	Capitalism

Bourgeoisie	Relative poverty
Proletariat	Underclass
Class consciousness	Life chances
False consciousness	Social mobility
Class	Open system
Status group	Closed system
Power	Horizontal mobility
Dominant ideology	Vertical mobility
Objective method	Intergenerational mobility
Prestige	Intragenerational mobility
Esteem	Colonialism
Absolute poverty	Neocolonialism

World systems analysis	Multinational corporations
Dependency theory	Modernization
Globalization	Modernization theory

SELF-TEST

MODIFIED TRUE-FALSE QUESTIONS: If the statement below is true, write "true" in the space provided. If the statement is false, briefly correct the error.

1. In ancient Greece, slave status was permanent.

2. It is estimated that at the beginning of the twenty-first century, more than 27 million people around the world were still enslaved.

3. According to Daniel Rossides, the largest social class in the United States is the upper-middle class.

4. Unlike Karl Marx, Max Weber insisted that no single characteristic (such as class) totally defines a person's position within the stratification system.

5. Max Weber suggested that status is objectively determined by people's lifestyles, and therefore cannot diverge from economic class standing.

6. Social science research has found that inequality exists in all societies—even the simplest.

7. Conflict sociologists argue that stratification will inevitably lead to instability and to social change.

8. The objective method of measuring social class views class largely as a social rather than a statistical, category.

9. Federal tax programs and minimum wage laws, welfare programs, and work incentive programs have helped decrease the income gap between the rich and the poor in the United States during the last three decades.

10. A key factor in the feminization of poverty has been the increase in families with women as single heads of households.

11. William Julius Wilson notes that poverty neighborhoods have become increasingly marginal to the economic, social, and cultural life of the city. He sees this as a *jobless ghetto*, with the exodus of well-paid jobs.

12. Herbert Gans notes that the presence of poor people means that society's dirty work—physically dirty or dangerous, dead-end and underpaid, undignified and menial jobs—will be performed at low cost.

13. The global debt crisis has lessened the Third World dependency begun under colonialism, neocolonialism, and multinational investment.

14. In the developing world, it is easy to build strong trade unions in factories run by multinational corporations.

15. Karuna Chanana Ahmed, an anthropologist from India who has studied developing nations, calls Blacks the most exploited among oppressed people.

MULTIPLE-CHOICE QUESTIONS: In each of the following, select the phrase that best completes the statement.

1. The most extreme form of legalized social inequality for individuals or groups is
   a. slavery.
   b. open class systems.
   c. closed caste systems.
   d. caste systems.

2. The caste system is generally associated with
   a. Hinduism.
   b. Islam.
   c. Judaism.
   d. Buddhism.

3. In sociologist Daniel Rossides's model of the class system of the United States, the class representing the smallest proportion of the population is the
   a. upper class.
   b. upper-middle class.
   c. lower-middle class.
   d. lower class.

4. In Karl Marx's view, the destruction of the capitalist system will occur only if the working class first develops
   a. bourgeois consciousness.
   b. false consciousness.
   c. class consciousness.
   d. caste consciousness.

5. Which of the following were viewed by Weber as distinct components of stratification?
   a. conformity, deviance, and social control
   b. class, status, and power
   c. class, caste, and age
   d. class, prestige, and esteem

6. Which sociological perspective argues that stratification is universal and that social inequality is necessary so that people will be motivated to fill socially important positions?
   a. functionalist perspective
   b. conflict perspective
   c. interactionist perspective
   d. labeling perspective

7. __________ refers to the reputation that a specific person has earned within an occupation.
   a. Prestige
   b. Esteem
   c. Status
   d. Power

8. In 1997, about what percentage of the wealth of the United States was held by the richest fifth (or top 20 percent) of the population?
   a. 23 percent
   b. 38 percent
   c. 85 percent
   d. 75 percent

9. In central cities, about 49 percent of the underclass are
   a. Whites.
   b. Asians.
   c. Hispanics.
   d. African Americans.

10. Which sociologist has applied functionalist analysis to the existence of poverty and argues that various segments of society actually benefit from the existence of the poor?
   a. Émile Durkheim
   b. Max Weber
   c. Karl Marx
   d. Herbert Gans

11. A plumber whose father was a physician is an example of
   a. downward intergenerational mobility.
   b. upward intergenerational mobility.
   c. downward intragenerational mobility.
   d. upward intragenerational mobility.

12. In viewing the global economic system as divided between those nations who control wealth and those from whom capital is taken, sociologist Immanuel Wallerstein draws on the
   a. functionalist perspective.
   b. conflict perspective.
   c. interactionist perspective.
   d. dramaturgical approach.

13. Which of the following nations would Wallerstein classify as a core country within the world economic system?
   a. Germany
   b. South Korea
   c. Ireland
   d. Mexico

14. Which sociological perspective emphasizes that multinational corporations can actually help the developing nations of the world?
    a. functionalist perspective
    b. conflict perspective
    c. interactionist perspective
    d. labeling theory

15. Current modernization studies generally take a ____________ perspective: using various indicators, researchers show how societies are moving closer together despite traditional differences.
    a. dependency
    b. convergence
    c. labeling
    d. world systems

FILL-IN QUESTIONS: Fill in the blank spaces in the sentences below with the correct words. Where two or more words are required, there will be a corresponding number of blank spaces.

1. ______________ involves the ways in which one generation passes on social inequalities to the next, thereby producing groups of people arranged in rank order from low to high.

2. ______________ theorists believe that a differential system of rewards and punishments is necessary for the efficient operation of society.

3. In Karl Marx's view, a capitalist society has a ______________ ideology that serves the interests of the ruling class.

4. The key to the ______________ method of measuring social class is that the researcher makes a determination about an individual's class position.

5. From 1929 through 1970, the United States government's economic and tax policies seemed to shift income shares somewhat to the ______________. However, in the last three decades federal tax policies favored the ______________.

6. One commonly used measure of absolute poverty is the federal government's ______________ ______________, which serves as an official definition of which people are poor.

7. Since World War II, an increasing proportion of the poor people of the United States are women, many of whom are divorced or never married mothers. This alarming trend is known as the ______________ ______________ ______________.

8. Sociologist William Julius Wilson and other social scientists have used the term ______________ to describe the long-term poor who lack training and skills.

9. ______________ notes that it is functional for society to have poor people because the identification and punishment of the poor as deviants upholds the legitimacy of the conventional social norms and "mainstream" values regarding hard work, thrift, and honesty.

10. An open class system implies that the position of each individual is influenced by the person's ______________ status.

11. A woman who enters the paid labor force as a teacher's aide and eventually becomes superintendent of the school district experiences upward ______________ mobility.

12. The long reign of the British Empire over much of North America, parts of Africa, and India is an example of ______________ domination.

13. In a sense, dependency theory can be regarded as an application of the ______________ perspective on a global scale.

14. Viewed from a ______________ perspective, the combination of skilled technology and management provided by multinationals and the relatively cheap labor available in developing nations is ideal for a global enterprise.

15. Many sociologists are quick to note that terms such as modernization and development contain a (an) ______________ bias.

UNDERSTANDING SOCIAL POLICY: All the following questions are based on material that appears in the social policy section on Rethinking Welfare in North America and Europe. Write a brief answer to each question in the space provided below.

1. What is the Personal Responsibility and Work Opportunity Reconciliation Act?

2. Compare the commitment to social service programs in the United States with programs that exist in European nations.

3. Why do sociologists tend to view the debate over welfare throughout industrialized nations from a conflict perspective?

4. What is meant by "corporate welfare"?

DEFINITIONS OF KEY TERMS

Social inequality: A condition in which members of a society have a different amount of wealth, prestige, or power. (187)

Stratification: A structured ranking of entire groups of people that perpetuates unequal economic rewards and power in a society. (187)

Income: Salaries and wages. (187)

Wealth: An inclusive term encompassing all of a person's material assets, including land and other types of property. (187)

Ascribed status: A social position "assigned" to a person by society without regard for the person's unique talents or characteristics. (188)

Achieved status: A social position attained by a person largely through his or her own effort. (188)

Slavery: A system of enforced servitude in which people are legally owned by others and in which enslaved status is transferred from parents to children. (189)

Castes: Hereditary systems of rank, usually religiously dictated, tending to be fixed and immobile. (189)

Class system: A social ranking based primarily on economic position in which achieved characteristics can influence mobility. (189)

Capitalism: An economic system in which the means of production are largely in private hands, and the main incentive for economic activity is the accumulation of profits. (192)

Bourgeoisie: Karl Marx's term for the capitalist class, comprising the owners of the means of production. (192)

Proletariat: Karl Marx's term for the working class in a capitalist society. (192)

Class consciousness: In Karl Marx's view, a subjective awareness held by members of a class regarding their common vested interests and need for collective political action to bring about social change. (192)

False consciousness: A term used by Karl Marx to describe an attitude held by members of a class that does not accurately reflect its objective position. (193)

Class: A group of people who have a similar level of wealth and income. (193)

Status group: People who have the same prestige or lifestyle, independent of their class positions. (193)

Power: The ability to exercise one's will over others. (193)

Dominant ideology: A set of cultural beliefs and practices that help maintain powerful social, economic, and political interests. (195)

Objective method: A technique for measuring social class that assigns individuals to classes on the basis of criteria such as occupation, education, income, and place of residence. (196)

Prestige: The respect and admiration that an occupation holds in a society. (196)

Esteem: The reputation that a particular individual has earned within an occupation. (196)

Absolute poverty: A standard of poverty based on a minimum level of subsistence below which families should not be expected to live. (199)

Relative poverty: A floating standard of deprivation by which people at the bottom of a society, whatever their lifestyles, are judged to be disadvantaged in comparison with the nation as a whole. (199)

Underclass: Long-term poor people who lack training and skills. (201)

Life chances: People's opportunities to provide themselves with material goods, positive living conditions, and favorable life experiences. (203)

Social mobility: Movement of individuals or groups from one position of a society's stratification system to another. (204)

Open system: A social system in which the position of each individual is influenced by his or her achieved status. (204)

Closed system: A social system in which there is little or no possibility of individual mobility. (204)

Horizontal mobility: The movement of an individual from one social position to another of the same rank. (205)

Vertical mobility: The movement of a person from one social position to another of a different rank. (205)

Intergenerational mobility: Changes in the social position of children relative to their parents. (205)

Intragenerational mobility: Changes in a person's social position within his or her adult life. (205)

Colonialism: The maintenance of political, social, economic, and cultural dominance over a people by a foreign power for an extended period of time. (208)

Neocolonialism: Continuing dependence of former colonies on foreign countries. (208)

World systems analysis: A view of the global economic system as divided between certain industrialized nations who control wealth and developing countries who are controlled and exploited. (208)

Dependency theory: An approach that contends that industrialized nations continue to exploit developing countries for their own gain. (208)

Globalization: Globalization is the worldwide integration of government policies, cultures, social movements, and financial markets through trade and the exchange of ideas. (208)

Multinational corporations: Commercial organizations that, while headquartered in one country, own or control other corporations and subsidiaries throughout the world. (209)

Modernization: The far reaching process by which peripheral nations move from having traditional or less developed institutions to those characteristics of more developed societies. (211)

Modernization theory: A functionalist approach that proposes that modernization and development will gradually improve the lives of people in peripheral nations. (211)

ANSWERS TO SELF-TEST

Modified True-False Questions

1. Although slave status in ancient Greece could be inherited by succeeding generations, it was not necessarily permanent. (189)
2. True (190)
3. According to Daniel Rossides, the largest social class in the United States is the working class. (192)
4. True (193)
5. Max Weber suggested that status is subjectively determined by people's lifestyles and therefore can diverge from economic class standing. (193)
6. True (194)
7. True (196)
8. The objective method of measuring social class views class largely as a statistical category. (196)
9. While the salaries of highly skilled workers and professionals have continued to rise during the last three decades, and especially during the 1980s, the wages of less skilled workers have decreased when controlled for inflation. As a result, income inequality rose substantially from 1967 to the end of the century. (198)
10. True (201)
11. True (202)
12. True (203)
13. The global debt crisis has intensified the Third World dependency begun under colonialism, neocolonialism, and multinational investment. (208)
14. In the developing world, it is difficult to build strong trade unions in factories run by multinational corporations. (210)
15. Karuna Chanana Ahmed calls women the most exploited among oppressed people. (213)

Multiple-Choice Questions

1. a (189)
2. a (189)
3. a (190)
4. c (192)
5. b (193)
6. a (194)
7. b (196)
8. c (199)
9. d (202)
10. d (203)
11. a (205)
12. b (208)
13. a (208)
14. a (209)
15. b (212)

Fill-In Questions

1. Stratification (187)
2. Functionalist (194)
3. dominant (195)
4. objective (196)
5. poor; affluent (198)
6. poverty line (199)
7. feminization of poverty (201)
8. underclass (201)
9. Herbert Gans (203)
10. achieved (204)
11. intragenerational (205)
12. colonial (208)
13. conflict (208)
14. functionalist (209)
15. ethnocentric (211)

Understanding Social Policy: Rethinking Welfare in North America and Europe

1. In late 1996, in a historic shift in federal policy, President Bill Clinton signed the Personal Responsibility and Work Opportunity Reconciliation Act. This law, passed with strong congressional support, ended the long-standing federal guarantee of assistance to every poor family that meets eligibility requirements. It set a lifetime limit of five years of welfare for recipients, and required that all able-bodied adults work after two years of benefits. The federal government would give block grants to the states to use as they wish in assisting poor and needy residents, and it would permit states to experiment with ways to move people off welfare. (213)
2. Most industrialized nations devote higher proportions of their expenditures to housing, social security, welfare, and unemployment compensation than the United States does. Sociologist Greg Duncan found that a higher proportion of the poor escape poverty in Europe than in the United States. (214)
3. Sociologists tend to view the debate over welfare throughout industrialized nations from a conflict perspective in this way: the "haves" in positions of policy-making listen to the interests of other "haves," while the cries of the "have-nots" are drowned out. From a conflict perspective, the backlash against welfare recipients reflects deep fears and hostility toward the nation's urban and predominantly African American and Hispanic underclass. (214)
4. "Corporate welfare" represents the tax breaks, direct payments, and grants that the government makes to corporations. An example is the airline bailout bill, which benefited airline executives and shareholders, while relatively low-paid airline employees were laid off. (214)

CHAPTER

10 RACIAL AND ETHNIC INEQUALITY

KEY POINTS

Racial and Ethnic Groups: Sociologists frequently distinguish between **racial** and **ethnic groups**. The term racial group is used to describe a group that is set apart from others because of obvious physical differences. Whites, African Americans, and Asian Americans are all considered racial groups in the United States. Unlike racial groups, an ethnic group is set apart from others primarily because of its national origin or distinctive cultural patterns. In the United States, Puerto Ricans, Jews, and Polish Americans are all categorized as ethnic groups. (221)

Minority Groups: A **minority group** is a subordinate group whose members have significantly less control or power over their own lives than members of a dominant or majority group have over theirs. Sociologists have identified five basic properties of a minority group: (1) members share physical or cultural characteristics that distinguish them from the dominant group; (2) members experience unequal treatment; (3) membership in the group is not voluntary—people are born into the group; (4) minority group members have a strong sense of group solidarity; and (5) members generally marry others from the same group. (221)

Biological Significance and Social Construction of Race: Viewed from a biological perspective, the term race would refer to a genetically isolated group with distinctive gene frequencies, but it is impossible to scientifically define or identify such a group. **Social construction of race** refers to the process by which people come to define a group as a race based in part on physical characteristics, but also on historical, cultural, and economic factors. (223)

Prejudice: **Prejudice** is a negative attitude toward an entire category of people, often an ethnic or racial minority. One important and widespread form of prejudice is racism, the belief that one race is supreme and all others are innately inferior. When racism prevails in a society, members of subordinate groups generally experience prejudice, discrimination, and exploitation. (225)

Studying Race and Ethnicity: Viewing race from the macrolevel, functionalists observe that racial prejudice and discrimination serve positive functions for dominant groups, whereas conflict theorists see the economic structure as a central factor in the exploitation of minorities. The microlevel analysis of interactionist researchers stresses the manner in which everyday contact between people from different racial and ethnic backgrounds contributes to tolerance or leads to hostility. (229)

Patterns of Inter-group Relations: There are four identifiable **patterns** that describe typical **inter-group relations** as they occur in North America and throughout the world. **Amalgamation** describes the end result when a majority group and a minority group combine to form a new group. Through intermarriage over several generations, various groups in the society combine to form a new group. **Assimilation** is the process by which a person forsakes his or her own cultural tradition to become part of a different culture. Generally, it is practiced by a minority group member who wants to conform to the standards of the dominant group. **Segregation** refers to the physical separation of two groups of people in terms of residence, workplace, and social functions. Generally, it is imposed by a dominant group on a minority group. **Pluralism** is based on mutual respect between various groups in a society for one another's cultures. It allows a minority group to express its own culture, and to still participate without prejudice in the larger society. (231)

African Americans: African Americans are the largest racial minority in the United States, but they have long been treated as second-class citizens. Currently, by the standards of the federal government, nearly 1 out of every 4 Blacks, as opposed to 1 out of every 11 Whites, is poor. Contemporary institutional discrimination and individual prejudice against African Americans are rooted in the history of slavery in the United States. During the decade of the 1960s, a vast civil rights movement emerged with many competing factions and strategies for change. There have been economic gains for some African Americans, especially middle-class men and women, over the last 35 years. (233)

Native Americans: There are approximately 2 million Native Americans. They represent a diverse array of cultures, distinguishable by language, family organization, religion, and livelihood. Today, life remains difficult for members of the 554 tribal groups in the United States, whether they live in cities or on reservations. By the 1990s, an increasing number of people in the United States were openly claiming an identity as Native American. Since 1960, the federal government's count of Native Americans has tripled to an estimated 1.8 million. (235)

Asian Americans: Asian Americans are held up as a model or ideal minority group, supposedly because despite suffering from prejudice and discrimination, they have succeeded economically, socially, and educationally without resorting to confrontations with Whites. This concept of a model minority ignores the diversity among Asian Americans: there are rich and poor Japanese Americans, rich and poor Filipino Americans, and so forth. The existence of a model minority seems to reaffirm the notion that anyone can get ahead in the United States with talent and hard work and implies that those minorities that don't succeed are somehow responsible for their failures. Viewed from a conflict perspective, this becomes yet another instance of "blaming the victims." (237)

Hispanics—an Overview: The various groups included under the general terms Hispanics and Latinos together represent the largest ethnic minority in the United States. The various Hispanic groups share a heritage of Spanish language and culture, which can cause serious problems for assimilation in the United States. The educational difficulties of Hispanic students certainly contribute to the generally low economic status of Hispanics. (239)

Jewish Americans: Jews have not achieved equality in the United States. Despite high levels of education and professional training, they are still conspicuously absent from the top management of large corporations (except for the few firms founded by Jews). As is true for other minorities, **Jewish Americans** face the choice of maintaining ties to their long religious and cultural heritage, or becoming as indistinguishable as possible from gentiles. A 1994 tabulation by the Anti-Defamation League (ADL), indicated that anti-Semitic acts reached the highest level in the 17 years during which the ADL has been recording such incidents. (242)

Global Immigration: Worldwide **immigration** is at an all-time high. Countries like the United States, which have long been a destination for immigrants, have a history of policies to determine who has preference to enter. Conflict theorists note how much of the debate over immigration is phrased in economic terms. Often, clear racial and ethnic biases are built into these policies. Immigration provides many valuable functions for the receiving society, but conflict theorists note how recent immigrants, primarily poor and Hispanic, are being firmly entrenched at the bottom of the nation's social and economic hierarchies. (243)

KEY TERMS

Briefly define or identify the following terms in the spaces provided below. The definitions of these terms can be found later in this chapter of the study guide.

Racial group	Ethnocentrism
Ethnic group	Racism
Minority group	Discrimination
Stereotypes	Glass ceiling
Prejudice	Institutional discrimination

Affirmative action	Pluralism
Exploitation theory	Black power
Contact hypothesis	Model or ideal minority
Genocide	Issei
Amalgamation	Nisei
Assimilation	Anti-Semitism
Segregation	Symbolic ethnicity
Apartheid	

SELF-TEST

MODIFIED TRUE-FALSE QUESTIONS: If the statement below is true, write "true" in the space provided. If the statement is false, briefly correct the error.

1. When sociologists define a minority group, they are primarily concerned with the economic and political power, or powerlessness, of that group.

2. The one-drop rule was a vivid example of the biological construction of race.

3. When allowed to check off multiple racial categories on the 2000 census, 7 million people reported that they were of two or more races.

4. Stratification along racial lines is more subject to change than stratification along ethnic lines.

5. A White corporate president with a completely respectful view of Vietnamese Americans refuses to hire such people for executive posts out of fear that biased clients will take their business elsewhere. The president's action constitutes prejudice without discrimination.

6. “Arab Americans” and “Muslims” can be bumped together as the same group.

7. In early 1995, the federal Glass Ceiling Commission found that affirmative action has completely eliminated glass ceilings and allowed women and minority group men to win a significant proportion of top management positions in the nation's industries.

8. Computer technology represents another area of institutional discrimination. Asian Americans are much less likely to have a computer in their home than Whites.

9. Affirmative action refers to hiring women and minorities for job openings and admitting members of these groups to college regardless of their competency.

10. Both the enslavement of Blacks and the extermination and removal westward of Native Americans were, to a significant extent, economically motivated.

11. The term genocide has been used in reference to the killing of 1 million Armenians by Turkey beginning in 1915.

12. Great Britain is an example of a nation that has been notably successful in achieving cultural pluralism in a multiracial society.

13. During World War II, the federal government decreed that all German Americans on the east coast leave their homes and report to "evacuation camps."

14. Politically, Puerto Ricans in the United States have been more successful than Mexican Americans in organizing for their rights.

15. Despite high levels of education and professional training, Jewish Americans are still conspicuously absent from the top management of large corporations (except for the few firms founded by Jews).

MULTIPLE-CHOICE QUESTIONS: In each of the following, select the phrase that best completes the statement.

1. Which of the following is considered a racial group?
   a. Mexican Americans
   b. Jewish Americans
   c. African Americans
   d. all of the above

2. Which of the following is considered an ethnic group?
   a. Puerto Ricans
   b. Jews
   c. Polish Americans
   d. all of the above

3. Which sociologist, writing in 1906, noted that individuals make distinctions between members of their own group (the in-group) and everyone else (the out-group)?
   a. Charles Horton Cooley
   b. Émile Durkheim
   c. William I. Thomas
   d. William Graham Sumner

4. The largest racial minority in the United States is
   a. Asians Americans.
   b. African Americans.
   c. Native Americans.
   d. Jewish Americans.

5. At one time, many Puerto Ricans were effectively barred from serving in the Chicago Police Department because they failed to meet a height requirement. This was an example of
   a. prejudice.
   b. scapegoating.
   c. a self-fulfilling prophecy.
   d. institutional discrimination.

6. Which sociological perspective views race from the macrolevel and sees the economic structure as a central factor in the exploitation of minority groups?
   a. functionalist perspective
   b. conflict perspective
   c. interactionist perspective
   d. labeling theory

7. A Hispanic woman and a Jewish man, working together as computer programmers for an electronics firm, overcome their initial prejudices and come to appreciate each other's strengths and talents. This is an example of
   a. the contact hypothesis.
   b. a self-fulfilling prophecy.
   c. amalgamation.
   d. reverse discrimination.

8. Which equation can be used to represent amalgamation?
   a. A + B + C = A
   b. A + B + C = A + B + C
   c. A + B + C = D
   d. A + B + C = A + B + D

9. Which equation can be used to represent pluralism?
   a. A + B + C = A
   b. A + B + C = A + B + C
   c. A + B + C = D
   d. A + B + C = A + B + D

10. Which Black person wrote the acclaimed novel *Invisible Man*?
    a. Malcolm X
    b. James Baldwin
    c. Alice Walker
    d. Ralph Ellison

11. The approximately 2 million Native Americans represent a diverse array of cultures distinguishable by
    a. language.
    b. family organization.
    c. religion.
    d. all of the above

12. The "model minority" stereotype of Asian Americans contains an implicit critique of Blacks, Hispanics, and others for failing to succeed as well as the model minority has. Which sociological perspective would view this as yet another instance of "blaming the victim"?
    a. functionalist perspective
    b. conflict perspective
    c. interactionist perspective
    d. dramaturgical approach

13. The largest Hispanic population of the United States is composed of
    a. Mexican Americans.
    b. Puerto Ricans.
    c. Cuban Americans.
    d. refugees from Central America.

14. Which country has the world's largest concentration of Jews?
    a. Israel
    b. Russia
    c. the United States
    d. Poland

15. The largest population of White ethnics in the United States consists of
    a. Italian Americans.
    b. Irish Americans.
    c. Polish Americans.
    d. German Americans.

FILL-IN QUESTIONS: Fill in the blank spaces in the sentences below with the correct words. Where two or more words are required, there will be a corresponding number of blank spaces.

1. Sociologists consider race and ethnicity to be ________________ statuses, since people are born into racial and ethnic groups.

2. Writing from the ________________ perspective, sociologist William I. Thomas observed that people respond not only to the objective features of a situation or person, but also to the meaning that situation or person has for them.

3. An ______________ person judges other cultures by the standards of his or her own group, which leads quite easily into prejudice against cultures viewed as inferior.

4. The largest group of Muslims in the United States is ______________ Americans.

5. Although racial discrimination may serve the interests of the powerful, such unequal treatment can also be ______________ to a society and even to its dominant group.

6. The microlevel analysis of the ______________ perspective stresses the manner in which everyday contact between people from different racial and ethnic backgrounds contributes to tolerance or leads to hostility.

7. Sociologists such as Oliver Cox and Robert Blauner have used the ______________ theory to explain the basis of racial subordination in the United States.

8. In the United States, there are Italian Americans, Polish Americans, Hispanics, and Jews who have changed their names to names typically found among White, Protestant families. This is an example of ______________.

9. In 1994, a prominent Black activist, ______________ ______________, was elected as South Africa's president in the nation's first election in which Blacks were allowed to vote.

10. The "______________ ______________" laws of the southern United States, designed to enforce official segregation, were upheld as constitutional by the Supreme Court in 1896.

11. In the 1960s, proponents of ______________ ______________ rejected the goal of assimilation into White, middle-class society. They defended the beauty and dignity of Black and African cultures and supported the creation of Black-controlled political and economic institutions.

12. One ______________ American teenager in six has attempted suicide—a rate four times higher than the rate for other teenagers.

13. During the 1992 Los Angeles riots, small businesses owned by ______________ Americans were a particular target.

14. The recent rapid growth of the Hispanic population has focused marketers' attention on the burgeoning Latino _______________ _______________.

15. White ethnic and racial minorities have often been antagonistic to one another because of economic competition—an interpretation in line with the _______________ approach to sociology.

UNDERSTANDING SOCIAL POLICY: All the following questions are based on material that appears in the social policy section on Global Immigration. Write a brief answer to each question in the space provided below.

1. What changes have occurred with respect to new immigrants to the United States since the 1960s?

2. What are the functions and dysfunctions of immigration?

3. What is the conflict theorists' view of immigration?

4. What is the Immigration Reform and Control Act of 1986 and what impact did it have?

DEFINITIONS OF KEY TERMS

Racial group: A group that is set apart from others because of obvious physical differences. (221)

Ethnic group: A group that is set apart from others because of its national origin or distinctive cultural patterns. (221)

Minority group: A subordinate group whose members have significantly less control or power over their lives than the members of a dominant or majority group have over theirs. (221)

Stereotypes: Unreliable generalizations about all members of a group that do not recognize individual differences within the group. (224)

Prejudice: A negative attitude toward an entire category of people, such as a racial or ethnic minority. (225)

Ethnocentrism: The tendency to assume that one's culture and way of life are superior to all others. (225)

Racism: The belief that one race is supreme and all others are innately inferior. (225)

Discrimination: The process of denying opportunities and equal rights to individuals and groups because of prejudice or for other arbitrary reasons. (225)

Glass ceiling: An invisible barrier that blocks the promotion of a qualified individual in a work environment because of the individual's gender, race, or ethnicity. (225)

Institutional discrimination: The denial of opportunities and equal rights to individuals or groups that results from the normal operation of a society. (227)

Affirmative action: Positive efforts to recruit minority group members or women for jobs, promotions, and educational opportunities. (228)

Exploitation theory: A Marxist theory that views racial subordination in the United States as a manifestation of the class system inherent in capitalism. (230)

Contact hypothesis: An interactionist perspective stating that interracial contact between people of equal status in noncompetitive circumstances will reduce prejudice. (230)

Genocide: The deliberate, systematic killing of an entire people or nation. (231)

Amalgamation: The process by which a majority group and a minority group combine through intermarriage to form a new group. (231)

Assimilation: The process by which a person forsakes his or her own cultural tradition to become part of a different culture. (232)

Segregation: The act of physically separating two groups, often imposed on a minority group by a dominant group. (232)

Apartheid: The policy of the South African government designed to maintain the separation of Blacks and other non-Whites from the dominant Whites. (232)

Pluralism: Mutual respect between the various groups in a society for one another's cultures, which allows minorities to express their own cultures without experiencing prejudice. (233)

Black power: A political philosophy promoted by many younger Blacks in the 1960s that supported the creation of Black-controlled political and economic institutions. (235)

Model or ideal minority: A group that, despite past prejudice and discrimination, succeeds economically, socially, and educationally without resorting to political or violent confrontations with Whites. (237)

Issei: The early Japanese immigrants to the United States. (238)

Nisei: Japanese born in the United States who were descendants of the Issei. (238)

Anti-Semitism: Anti-Jewish prejudice. (242)

Symbolic ethnicity: An ethnic identity that emphasizes such concerns as ethnic food and political issues rather than deeper ties to one's ethnic heritage. (243)

ANSWERS TO SELF-TEST

Modified True-False Questions

1. True (221)
2. The one-drop rule was a vivid example of the social construction of race. (223)
3. True (223)
4. Stratification along racial lines is less subject to change than stratification along ethnic lines. (224)
5. The president's action constitutes discrimination without prejudice. (225)
6. While these groups overlap, many Arab Americans are Christians, and many Muslims are non-Arabs. (226)
7. In early 1995, the federal Glass Ceiling Commission found that glass ceilings continue to block women and minority group men from top management positions in the nation's industries. (227)
8. African Americans are much less likely to have a computer in their home than are Whites. (228)
9. Affirmative action refers to positive efforts to recruit minority members or women for jobs, promotions, and educational opportunities. (228)
10. True (230)
11. True (231)
12. Great Britain is an example of a nation that has had difficulty achieving cultural pluralism in a multiracial society. (233)
13. During World War II, the federal government decreed that all Japanese Americans on the west coast leave their homes and report to "evacuation camps." (238)
14. Politically, Puerto Ricans in the United States have not been as successful as Mexican Americans in organizing for their rights. (240)
15. True (242)

Multiple-Choice Questions

1. c (221)
2. d (221)
3. d (222)
4. b (222)
5. d (227)
6. b (230)
7. a (230)
8. c (231)
9. b (233)
10. d (233)
11. d (235)
12. b (237)
13. a (240)
14. c (242)
15. d (242)

Fill-In Questions

1. ascribed (222)
2. interactionist (224)
3. ethnocentric (225)
4. African (226)
5. dysfunctional (230)
6. interactionist (230)
7. exploitation (230)
8. assimilation (232)
9. Nelson Mandela (232)
10. Jim Crow (233)
11. Black power (235)
12. Native (236)
13. Korean (239)
14. middle class (241)
15. conflict (243)

Understanding Social Policy: Global Immigration

1. Since the 1960s, policies in the United States have encouraged immigration of people with relatives here as well as people who have needed skills. The change has significantly altered the pattern of sending nations. Previously Europeans dominated, but for the last 40 years immigrants have come primarily from Latin America and Asia. (243)
2. Despite people's fears about it, immigration provides many valuable functions. For the receiving society it alleviates labor shortages, such as in the area of health care technology in the United States. For the sending nation, migration can relieve economies unable to support large numbers of people. Often overlooked is the large amount of money that immigrants send back to their home nations. When migrants with skills or educational potential leave developing countries, it can be dysfunctional for those nations. (244)
3. Conflict theorists note how much of the debate over immigration is phrased in economic terms. But this debate is intensified when the arrivals are of different racial and ethnic background than the host population. Fear and dislike of "new" ethnic groups divide countries throughout the world. (244)
4. The Immigration Reform and Control Act of 1986 marked a historic change in immigration policy. Hiring of illegal aliens was outlawed, and employers caught violating the law became subject to fines and even prison sentences. Just as significant a change was the extension of amnesty and legal status to many illegal immigrants already living in the United States. Critics of the law emphasize its devastating impact on those illegal immigrants who could not qualify for amnesty. Many aliens in this situation are being overworked or underpaid by unscrupulous employers who are well aware that these workers have few options. (245)

CHAPTER

11 STRATIFICATION BY GENDER AND AGE

KEY POINTS

Social Construction of Gender: In studying gender, sociologists are interested in the gender-role socialization that leads females and males to behave differently. The application of traditional gender roles leads to many forms of differentiation between women and men. Gender roles are evident not only in our work and behavior but in how we react to others. We are constantly "doing gender" without realizing it. We socially construct our behavior so that male-female differences are either created or exaggerated. (251)

Gender Role Socialization in the United States: According to traditional gender-role patterns that have been influential in the socialization of children in the United States, boys must be masculine (active, aggressive, tough, daring, and dominant), whereas girls must be feminine (soft, emotional, sweet, and submissive). It is adults, of course, who play a critical role in guiding children into those gender roles deemed appropriate in a society. Parents are normally the first and most crucial agents of socialization. But other adults, older siblings, the mass media, and religious and educational institutions also exert an important influence on gender role socialization in the United States. (252)

The Functionalist View of Gender Stratification: Functionalists maintain that gender differentiation has contributed to overall social stability. Sociologists Talcott Parsons and Robert Bales argue that in order to function most efficiently, the family requires adults who will specialize in particular roles. They contend that women take the expressive, emotionally supportive role, and men take the instrumental, practical role, with the two roles complementing each other. Parsons and Bales do not explicitly endorse traditional gender roles, but they imply that a division of tasks between spouses is functional for the family unit. (255)

The Conflict View of Gender Stratification: Conflict theorists see gender differences as a reflection of the subjugation of one group (women) by another group (men). If we use an analogy to Marx's analysis of class conflict, we can say that males are like the bourgeois, or capitalists; they control most of the society's wealth, prestige, and power. Females are like the proletariat, or workers; they can acquire valuable resources only by following the dictates of their "bosses." (255)

The Feminist Perspective: A significant component of the conflict approach to gender stratification draws on feminist theory. Feminist sociologists would find little to disagree with in the conflict theorists' perspective. But the feminist perspective would argue that the very discussion of women and society, however well meaning, has been distorted by the exclusion of women from academic thought, including sociology. For most of the history of sociology, studies were conducted on male subjects or about male-led groups and organizations, and the findings were generalized to all people. (256)

The Interactionist View of Gender Stratification: While functionalists and conflict theorists studying gender stratification typically focus on macrolevel social forces and institutions, interactionist researchers often examine gender stratification on the microlevel of everyday behavior. For example, men are more likely than women to change topics of conversation, to ignore topics chosen by members of the opposite sex, to minimize the contributions and ideas of members of the opposite sex, and to validate their own contributions. These patterns reflect the conversational (and, in a sense, political) dominance of males. From an interactionist perspective, day-to-day cross-sex conversations are one more battleground in the struggle for sexual equality—as women try to "get a word in edgewise" in the midst of men's interruptions and verbal dominance. (256)

Women—the Oppressed Majority: When one looks at the political structure of the United States, women remain noticeably underrepresented. No woman has ever served as president of the United States, vice president, speaker of the House of Representatives, or chief justice of the Supreme Court. This lack of women in decision-making positions is evidence of women's powerlessness in the United States. If we apply the model of a minority or subordinate group to the situation of women in this country, we find that a numerical majority group fits our definition of a subordinate minority. Women can be said to suffer both from individual acts of sexism (such as sexist remarks and acts of violence) and from institutional sexism. All the major institutions of our society are controlled by men. These institutions, in their "normal," day-to-day operations, often discriminate against women and perpetuate sexism. (257)

The Status of Women Worldwide: Women experience second-class treatment throughout the world. They constitute one-third of the world's paid labor force, but are generally found in the lowest-paying jobs. Single-parent households headed by women, which appear to be on the increase in many nations, are typically found in the poorest sections of the population. Indeed, the feminization of poverty has become a global phenomenon. While the situation of women in Sweden and the United States is significantly better than in Saudi Arabia and Bangladesh, women nevertheless remain in a second-class position in the world's most affluent and developed countries. (258)

Women in the Work Force of the United States: Women's participation in the paid labor force increased steadily throughout the twentieth century. A majority of women are now members of the paid labor force, not full-time homemakers. Unfortunately, women entering the job market find their options restricted in important ways. Particularly damaging to women workers is occupational segregation, or confinement to sex-typed "women's jobs." Women earn much less money than men do in the paid labor force of the United States. Women from all groups and men from minority groups sometimes encounter attitudinal or organizational bias that prevents them from reaching their full potential. The glass ceiling refers to an invisible barrier that blocks the promotion of a qualified individual in a work environment. (261)

Social Consequences of Women's Employment: Studies indicate that there continues to be a clear gender gap in the performance of housework, although the differences are narrowing. The most recent study finds women doing more housework and spending more time on child care than men, whether it be on a workday or when off work. Sociologist Arlie Hochschild has used the phrase "second shift" to describe the double burden that many women face and few men share equitably: working outside the home followed by childcare and housework. (262)

Women—the Emergence of a Collective Consciousness: The feminist movement of the United States was born in Seneca Falls, New York in the summer of 1848. Ultimately, the early feminists won many victories, among them the passage and ratification of the Nineteenth Amendment to the Constitution, which granted women the right to vote in national elections beginning in 1920. The second wave of feminism in the United States emerged in the 1960s and came into full force in the 1970s. A sense of "sisterhood," much like the class-consciousness that Marx hoped would emerge in the proletariat became evident. Individual women identified their interests with those of the collectivity women. No longer were they "happy" in submissive, subordinate roles ("false consciousness" in Marxist terms). (264)

Aging and Society: "Being old" is a master status that commonly overshadows all others in the United States. Once people are labeled "old," this designation has a major impact on how others perceive them, and even on how they view themselves. Negative stereotypes of the elderly contribute to their position as a minority group subject to discrimination. The elderly experience unequal treatment in employment and may face prejudice and discrimination: they share physical characteristics that distinguish them from younger people; their membership in a disadvantaged minority is involuntary; they have a strong sense of group solidarity; and they are generally married to others of a comparable age. (265)

Disengagement Theory: Elaine Cumming and William Henry introduced an explanation of the impact of aging during one's life course known as **disengagement theory**. This theory contends that society and the aging individual mutually sever many of their relationships. In keeping with the functionalist perspective, disengagement theory emphasizes that passing social roles on from one generation to another ensures social stability. Implicit in disengagement theory is the view that society should help older people withdraw from their accustomed social roles. Although functionalist in its approach, disengagement theory ignores the fact that postretirement employment has been increasing in recent decades. (266)

Activity Theory: Often seen as an opposing approach to disengagement theory, **activity theory** argues that the elderly person who remains active will be best adjusted. Proponents of activity theory view older people's withdrawal from society as harmful for both the elderly and society, and focuses on the potential contributions of older people to the maintenance of society. In their opinion, aging citizens will feel satisfied only when they can be useful and productive in society's terms, primarily by working for wages. (267)

The Conflict Approach: Conflict theorists have criticized both disengagement theory and activity theory for failing to consider the impact of social structure on patterns of aging. According to the conflict approach, the treatment of older people in the United States reflects the many divisions in our society. The low status of older people is seen in prejudice and discrimination against them, age segregation, and unfair job practices—none of which are directly addressed by either disengagement theory or activity theory. (268)

The "Graying of America": An increasing proportion of the population of the United States is composed of older people. Men and women aged 65 years and over constituted only 4 percent of the national population in the year 1900, but by 2001 this figure had reached 24 percent. While the United States is noticeably graying, the nation's older citizens are in a sense getting younger due to improved health and nutrition. As a group, older people in the United States are neither homogeneous nor poor. The typical elderly person enjoys a standard of living that is much higher than at any point in the nation's past. (269)

Ageism: Physician Robert Butler coined the term "ageism" to refer to prejudice and discrimination against the elderly. Ageism reflects a deep uneasiness among young and middle-aged people about growing old. For many, old age symbolizes disease, disability, and death; seeing the elderly serves as a reminder that they may someday become old and infirm. (270)

Theory of Cumulative Disadvantage: The cumulative disadvantage theory supports the ideology that those who are advantaged early in life have more of an opportunity to receive formal schooling, to obtain a job that leads to advancement, to save for retirement, and to have access to dependable retirement programs. The advantages accumulate over the life course, while the disadvantages suffered by racial and ethnic groups accumulate. (271)

The Elderly—Emergence of a Collective Consciousness: In the 1970s, many older people became aware that they were being treated as second-class citizens, and they turned to collective action. The largest organization representing the nation's elderly is the American Association of Retired Persons (AARP), founded in 1958 by a retired school principal who was having difficulty getting insurance because of age prejudice. The potential power of the AARP is enormous; it is the third-largest voluntary association in the United States (behind only the Roman Catholic church and the American Automobile Association), and represents one out of every four registered voters in the United States. (272)

The Battle over Abortion from a Global Perspective: A critical victory for the struggle for legalized abortion in the United States came in 1973 when the Supreme Court granted women the right to terminate pregnancies in the *Roe v. Wade* ruling. The debate that has followed *Roe v. Wade* revolves around prohibiting abortion altogether, or at the very least, putting limits on it. In 1979, for example, Missouri required parental consent for minors wishing to obtain an abortion, and the Supreme Court upheld this law. Sociologists see gender and social class as largely defining the issues surrounding abortion. In terms of social class, the first major restriction on the legal right to terminate a pregnancy affected poor people. In 1976, Congress passed the Hyde Amendment, which banned the use of Medicaid and other federal funds for abortions. Viewed from a conflict perspective, this is one more financial burden that falls especially heavily on low-income women. Increasingly, pro-choice advocates are turning to the state courts for favorable decisions on the right to an abortion. In 1999, the U.S. House of Representatives passed the Unborn Victims of Violence Act, which elevates all stages of prenatal development, even an embryo, to the legal standing of a person. A presidential veto and Supreme Court rejection of the legislation are both likely. (273)

KEY TERMS

Briefly define or identify the following terms in the spaces provided below. The definitions of these terms can be found later in this chapter of the study guide.

Gender roles	Sexual harassment
Homophobia	Glass ceiling
Instrumentality	Second shift
Expressiveness	Gerontology
Sexism	Disengagement theory
Institutional discrimination	Activity theory

Ageism	

SELF-TEST

MODIFIED TRUE-FALSE QUESTIONS: If the statement below is true, write "true" in the space provided. If the statement is false, briefly correct the error.

1. Gender roles are biologically determined.

2. Homophobia significantly reduces rigid gender-role socialization.

3. The research of anthropologist Margaret Mead points to the importance of biological factors in defining the social roles of males and females.

4. Conflict theorists see gender differences as a reflection of the subjugation of one group (women) by another group (men).

5. Sociologists associated with the interactionist approach generally agree with the conflict perspective that men hold a dominant position over women.

6. In 2000, women accounted for 50 percent of all secretaries and dental assistants and 34 percent of all librarians.

7. A study done by the General Accounting Office in 2002 compared managerial salaries for men and women in 10 different industries, and found that on average women earned only about 78 cents for every dollar earned by men.

8. As married women have taken on more and more hours of paid employment, they have been extremely successful in getting their husbands to assume a greater role in needed homemaking duties.

9. The first wave of feminism in the United States emerged in the 1960s and came into full force in the 1970s.

10. A sense of "sisterhood," much like the false consciousness that Marx hoped would emerge in the proletariat, became evident in the feminist movement of the 1960s and 1970s.

11. Unlike gender, age is an achieved status that forms the basis for social differentiation.

12. Gerontologists rely heavily on sociological principles to explain the impact of aging on the individual and society.

13. Conflict theorists have noted that as societies make the transition from agricultural economies to industrialization and capitalism, the importance of older people within the economy tends to increase.

14. The theory of cumulative disadvantage suggests that people who suffered disadvantages based on their ethnic and racial backgrounds throughout their lives will suffer from greater disadvantages during old age, too.

15. Younger adults continue to view older workers as "job stealers," a biased judgment similar to that directed against illegal immigrants.

MULTIPLE-CHOICE QUESTIONS: In each of the following, select the phrase that best completes the statement.

1. The most crucial agent of socialization in teaching gender roles in the United States is
   a. peers.
   b. teachers.
   c. media personalities.
   d. parents.

2. Which of the following is not a component of the male gender role as outlined by Robert Brannon and James Doyle?
   a. success element: prove one's masculinity at work and sports
   b. aggressive element: use force in dealing with others
   c. subordination element: place one's needs after those of spouse and children
   d. self-reliant element: keep cool and unflappable

3. In which culture of New Guinea were expectations of each sex almost the reverse of those found in the United States?
   a. Arapesh
   b. Mundugumor
   c. Tchambuli
   d. Klingons

4. Which sociological perspective emphasizes that the relationship between females and males has been one of unequal power, with men in a dominant position over women?
   a. functionalist perspective
   b. conflict perspective
   c. interactionist perspective
   d. dramaturgical perspective

5. Which sociological perspective makes the distinction between instrumental and expressive roles?
   a. functionalist perspective
   b. conflict perspective
   c. interactionist perspective
   d. labeling theory

6. In studying gender stratification, which sociological perspective typically focuses on the microlevel of everyday behavior, such as cross-sex conversation?
   a. functionalist perspective
   b. conflict perspective
   c. interactionist perspective
   d. each of the above

7. The courts recognize two kinds of sexual harassment:
   a. quid pro quo and a hostile environment.
   b. squid con so and a hostile environment.
   c. quid pro con and a hostile environment.
   d. none of the above

8. Which of the following statements about the status of women around the world is correct?
   a. Women rarely hold top executive positions.
   b. Women almost always work in occupations with lower status and pay than men.
   c. Many women work as unpaid family laborers.
   d. all of the above

9. Which sociologist has used the phase "second shift" to describe the double burden—work outside the home followed by child care and housework—that many women face and few men share equitably?
   a. Heidi Hartmann
   b. Arlie Hochschild
   c. Talcott Parsons
   d. Kristin Luker

10. The sense of "sisterhood" that became evident during the rise of the contemporary feminist movement resembled the Marxist concept of
    a. alienation.
    b. dialectics.
    c. class consciousness.
    d. false consciousness.

11. Which one of the following statements about the elderly is correct?
    a. Being old is a master status.
    b. Once people are labeled as old, it has a major impact on how others perceive them.
    c. Once people are labeled as old, it has a major impact on how people view themselves.
    d. all of the above

12. What is the one crucial difference between older people and other subordinate groups, such as racial and ethnic minorities or women?
    a. Older people do not experience unequal treatment in employment.
    b. Older people have a strong sense of group solidarity and other groups do not.
    c. All of us who live long enough will eventually assume the ascribed status of being an older person.
    d. Older people are generally married to others of comparable age and other minorities do not marry within their group.

13. Which sociological perspective is most likely to emphasize the important role of social networks in providing life satisfaction for the elderly?
    a. functionalist perspective
    b. conflict perspective
    c. interactionist perspective
    d. labeling theory

14. Which sociological perspective views the treatment of older people as reflective of the many divisions in our society?
    a. functionalist perspective
    b. conflict perspective
    c. interactionist perspective
    d. labeling theory

15. Which sociological viewpoint emphasizes that older women experience a double burden, as do older members of racial and ethnic minority groups?
    a. functionalist perspective
    b. theory of cumulative disadvantage
    c. interactionist perspective
    d. labeling theory

FILL-IN QUESTIONS: Fill in the blank spaces in the sentences below with the correct words. Where two or more words are required, there will be a corresponding number of blank spaces.

1. ______________ contributes significantly to rigid gender-role socialization, since many people stereotypically associate male homosexuality with femininity and lesbianism with masculinity.

2. In Margaret Mead's analysis of New Guinea tribes, she indicated that among the ______________ both men and women act the way we would expect women to act—in a mild, parental, responsive way.

3. Within the general framework of their theory, ______________ sociologists maintain that gender differentiation has contributed to overall social stability.

4. Talcott Parsons and Robert Bales contend that women take the ______________, emotionally supportive role in the family and men take the ______________, practical role.

5. ______________ theorists would say males are like the bourgeoisie, or capitalists (they control most of the society's wealth, prestige, and power), and females are like the proletariat, or workers.

6. Studies show that up to 96 percent of all interruptions in cross-sex (male-female) conversations are initiated by ______________.

7. It is not simply that particular men in the United States are biased in their treatment of women. All the major institutions of our society—including the government, armed forces, large corporations, the media, the universities, and the medical establishment—are controlled by men. This situation is symptomatic of institutional ______________.

8. Women from all groups and men from minority groups sometimes encounter attitudinal or organizational bias that prevents them from reaching their full potential. This is known as the ______________ ______________.

9. Sociologist Arlie Hochschild has used the phrase "______________ ______________" to describe the double burden that many women face and few men share equitably: working outside the home followed by childcare and housework.

10. The ______________ Amendment to the Constitution granted women the right to vote in national elections beginning in 1920.

11. In keeping with the ______________ perspective of sociology, disengagement theory emphasizes that a society's stability is ensured when social roles are passed on from one generation to another.

12. The improved health of older people, which is sometimes overlooked by social scientists, has strengthened the arguments of ______________ theorists regarding how society should deal with the elderly.

13. ______________ theorists argue that both the disengagement and the activity perspectives often ignore the impact of social class in the lives of the elderly.

14. A critical victory in the struggle for legalized abortion in the United States came in 1973 when the Supreme Court granted women the right to terminate pregnancies in the ______________ v. ______________ decision.

15. The Supreme Court currently supports the general right to terminate a pregnancy by a narrow ______________.

UNDERSTANDING SOCIAL POLICY: All the following questions are based on material that appears in the social policy section on The Battle Over Abortion from a Global Perspective. Write a brief answer to each question in the space provided below.

1. What is at the heart of the abortion controversy in the United States today?

2. In what way has changing technology had an impact on the abortion controversy?

3. What is the sociological interest in abortion rights?

4. In the battle between pro-choice and pro-life activists, what are the most recent policy initiatives that have been made with respect to abortion rights in the United States?

DEFINITIONS OF KEY TERMS

Gender roles: Expectations regarding the proper behavior, attitudes, and activities of males and females. (251)

Homophobia: Fear of and prejudice against homosexuality. (252)

Instrumentality: A term used to refer to emphasis on tasks, focus on more distant goals, and a concern for the external relationship between one's family and other social institutions. (255)

Expressiveness: A term used to refer to concern for maintenance of harmony and the internal emotional affairs of the family. (255)

Sexism: The ideology that one sex is superior to the other. (257)

Institutional discrimination: The denial of opportunities and equal rights to individuals and groups resulting from the normal operations of a society. (257)

Sexual Harassment: Sexual Harassment is behavior that occurs when work benefits are made contingent on sexual favors, or when touching, lewd comments, or the appearance of pornographic material creates a "hostile environment" in the workplace. (258)

Glass ceiling: An invisible barrier that blocks the promotion of a qualified individual in a work environment because of the individual's gender, race, or ethnicity. (261)

Second shift: The double burden of work outside the home followed by child care and housework that many women face. (263)

Gerontology: The scientific study of the sociological and psychological aspects of aging and the problems of the aged. (266)

Disengagement theory: A functionalist theory of aging contending that society and the aging individual mutually sever many of their relationships. (266)

Activity theory: An interactionist theory of aging that argues that elderly people who remain active will be best adjusted. (267)

Ageism: A term used to refer to prejudice and discrimination against the elderly. (270)

ANSWERS TO SELF-TEST

Modified True-False Questions

1. We socially construct our behavior so that male-female differences are either created or exaggerated. (252)
2. Homophobia contributes significantly to rigid gender-role socialization. (252)
3. The research of anthropologist Margaret Mead points to the importance of cultural conditioning—as opposed to biological factors—in defining the social roles of males and females. (254)
4. True (255)
5. True (257)
6. In 2000, women accounted for 98 percent of all secretaries, 99 percent of all dental assistants and 85 percent of all librarians. (261)
7. True (262)
8. As married women have taken on more and more hours of paid employment, they have been only partially successful in getting their husbands to assume a greater role in needed homemaking duties. (263)
9. The first wave of feminism in the United States emerged in the mid-1800s; the second wave emerged in the 1960s and came into full force in the 1970s. (264)
10. A sense of "sisterhood," much like the class consciousness that Marx hoped would emerge in the proletariat, became evident in the feminist movement of the 1960s and 1970s. (264)
11. Like gender, age is an ascribed status that forms the basis for social differentiation. (266)
12. True (266)
13. Conflict theorists have noted that as societies make the transition from agricultural economies to industrial societies and capitalism, the importance of older people within the economy tends to erode. (268)
14. True (271)
15. True (271)

Multiple-Choice Questions

1. d (252)
2. c (253)
3. c (254)
4. b (255)
5. a (255)
6. c (256)
7. a (258)
8. d (260)
9. b (263)
10. c (264)
11. d (266)
12. c (266)
13. c (267)
14. b (268)
15. b (271)

Fill-In Questions

1. Homophobia (252)
2. Arapesh (254)
3. functionalist (255)
4. expressive; instrumental (255)
5. conflict (255)
6. men (257)
7. discrimination (258)
8. glass ceiling (261)
9. second shift (263)
10. Nineteenth (264)
11. functionalist (267)
12. activity (267)
13. Conflict (268)
14. Roe, Wade (273)

15. 5-4 majority (275)

Understanding Social Policy: The Battle Over Abortion

1. A critical victory in the struggle for legalized abortion in the United States came in 1973 in the Supreme Court case of *Roe v. Wade*, which was based on a woman's right to privacy. The Court's decision was generally applauded by pro-choice groups, which believe women have the right to make their own decisions about their bodies and should have access to safe and legal abortions. However, for pro-life groups, abortion is a moral and often religious issue. In their view, human life actually begins at the moment of conception rather than at the moment of a baby's delivery. Termination of this life is viewed as essentially an act of murder. (273)
2. "Day-after" pills are available in some nations; these pills can abort the fertilized egg the day after conception. In the United States, doctors, guided by ultrasound, can now end a pregnancy as early as eight days after conception. Pro-life activists are concerned that the use of this ultrasound technology will allow people to terminate pregnancies of unwanted females in nations where a premium is placed on male offspring. (274)
3. Sociologists view gender and social class as largely defining the issues surrounding abortion. The intense conflict over abortion reflects broader differences over women's position in society. Feminists involved in defending abortion rights typically believe that men and women are essentially similar; they support women's full participation in work outside the home and oppose all forms of sex discrimination. By contrast, most anti-abortion activists believe that men and women are fundamentally different. In their view, men are best suited for the public world of work, whereas women are best suited for the demanding and crucial task of rearing children. These activists are troubled by women's growing participation in work outside the home, which they view as destructive to the family and ultimately to society as a whole. (274)
4. The Supreme Court currently supports the general right to terminate a pregnancy by a narrow 5-4 majority. While pro-life activists continue to hope for an overruling of *Roe v. Wade*, they have focused in the interim on weakening the decision through such issues as limiting the use of fetal tissue in medical experiments and prohibiting late-term abortions. In 1998 the Court gave the states authority to prohibit abortions at the point where the fetus is viable outside the mother's womb. (275)

CHAPTER 12 THE FAMILY AND INTIMATE RELATIONSHIPS

KEY POINTS

Composition: What Is the Family? A family can be defined as a set of people related by blood, marriage (or some other agreed-upon relationship), or adoption who share the primary responsibility for reproduction and caring for members of society. In the United States, the family has traditionally been viewed in very narrow terms as a married couple and their unmarried children living together. However, this is but one type of family—what sociologists refer to as a nuclear family. People in the United States see the **nuclear family** as the preferred form of family arrangement. By contrast, an **extended family** is a family in which relatives, in addition to parents and children, live in the same home. (281)

Kinship Patterns: To Whom Are We Related? The state of being related to others is called kinship. The United States follows the pattern of bilateral descent, which means that both sides of a person's family are regarded as equally important. **Patrilineal descent** indicates that only the father's relatives are important in determining property, inheritance, and emotional ties. Conversely, in societies that favor **matrilineal descent**, only the mother's relatives are significant. New forms of reproductive technology will force a new way of looking at kinship. Today, a combination of biological and social processes can "create" a family member, requiring that more distinctions be made about who is related to whom. (283)

Authority Patterns—Who Rules? Societies vary in the way that power within the family is distributed. If a society expects males to dominate in all family decision-making, it is termed a **patriarchy**. By contrast, in a **matriarchy**, women have greater authority than men. The third type of authority pattern, the **egalitarian family**, is one in which spouses are regarded as equals. This does not mean, however, that each decision is shared in such families. Wives may hold authority in some spheres; husbands in others. (283)

Functionalist View of the Family: There are six permanent functions performed by the family; they were first outlined a half-century ago by sociologist William F. Ogburn. These are (1) reproduction, (2) protection, (3) socialization, (4) regulation of sexual behavior, (5) affection and companionship, and (6) providing of social status. (284)

Conflict View of the Family: Conflict theorists view the family not as a contributor to social stability, but as a reflection of the inequality in wealth and power found within the larger society. Feminist theorists and conflict theorists note that the family has traditionally legitimized and perpetuated male dominance. While the egalitarian family has become a more common pattern in the United States in recent decades, male dominance within the family has hardly disappeared. Conflict theorists also view the family as an economic unit that contributes to societal injustice. Children "inherit" the privileged or less-than-privileged social and economic status of their parents. (284)

Interactionist View: Interactionists focus on the microlevel of family and other intimate relationships. They are interested in how individuals interact with one another: whether they are cohabiting partners or long-time married couples. Interactionists might, for example, study the relationship between parents and children in interracial marriages and in stepfamilies. (286)

Feminist View: The feminist view maintains that in any society, the family plays a central role in socializing children. Therefore, the degree to which society manifests sexism is rooted in the family—an institution, ironically, in which women's work is essential. The oppressive way in which most households are organized, then, serves to reinforce societal sexism. (286)

Parenthood and Grandparenthood: The socialization of children is essential to the maintenance of any culture. Consequently, parenthood is one of the most important (and most demanding) social roles in the United States. Sociologist Alice Rossi identified four factors that complicate the transition to parenthood and the role of socializer. First, there is little anticipatory socialization for the social role of caregiver. Second, only limited learning occurs during the period of pregnancy itself. Third, the transition to parenthood is quite abrupt. Finally, in Rossi's view, our society lacks clear and helpful guidelines for successful parenthood. (291)

Dual-Income Families: The expectation of a family consisting of a wage-earning husband with a wife who stays at home has largely given way to the dual-income household. Among married people between the ages of 25 and 34, 97 percent of the men and 71 percent of women are in the labor force. A major factor in the rise of dual-income couples is economic need. Other factors contributing to the rise of the dual-income model include the nation's declining birthrate, the increase in the proportion of women with a college education, the shift in the economy of the United States from manufacturing to service industries, and the impact of the feminist movement in changing women's consciousness. (292)

Single-Parent Families: In 2000, a single parent headed about 21 percent of White families with children under 18, 35 percent of Hispanic families with children, and 65 percent of African American families with children. A family headed by a single mother faces especially difficult problems when the mother is a teenager. While 82 percent of single parents in the United States are mothers, the number of households headed by single fathers more than quadrupled over the period from 1980 to 2000. (293)

Factors Associated with Divorce: Perhaps the most important factor in the increase in divorce throughout the twentieth century has been the greater social acceptance of divorce. Most importantly, various religious denominations have relaxed negative attitudes toward divorce, and most religious leaders no longer treat it as a sin. In addition, many states have adopted more liberal divorce laws, families have fewer children, more couples can afford divorces, and more and more women are becoming less economically dependent on their husbands. (295)

Cohabitation: One of the most dramatic trends of recent years has been the tremendous increase in male-female couples who choose to live together without marrying, thereby engaging in what is commonly called cohabitation. The number of such households in the United States rose sixfold in the 1960s and increased another 48 percent just between 1990 and 1998. Working couples are almost twice as likely to cohabit as college students, and half of all people involved in cohabitation in the United States have been previously married. Older people may choose cohabitation rather than marriage for many reasons: religious differences, to preserve full Social Security benefits, out of fear of commitment, to avoid upsetting children from previous marriages, because one or both partners are not legally divorced, or because one or both has lived through a spouse's illness and death and does not want to experience that again. (296)

Remaining Single: More and more people are postponing entry into first marriages. As of 2000, one out of every four households in the United States (accounting for over 26 million people) was a single member household. The trend toward maintaining a single lifestyle is related to the growing economic independence of young people. This is especially significant for women. Freed from financial needs, women don't necessarily have to marry to enjoy a satisfying life. (297)

Lesbian and Gay Relationships: The lifestyles of lesbians and gay men vary greatly. Some live in long-term monogamous relationships; some couples live with children from former heterosexual marriages or adopted children; some live alone, others with roommates; and others remain married and do not publicly acknowledge their homosexuality. The contemporary lesbian and gay rights movement has given an increasing number of lesbians and gay men the support to proclaim their sexual and affectional orientation. (298)

Reproductive Technology: In an effort to overcome infertility, many couples turn to a recent reproductive advance known as in vitro fertilization (IVF). Replacing personnel is a functional prerequisite that the family as a social institution performs. However, the conflict perspective would note that in the world today, the available technologies are often only accessible to the most affluent. Conflict theorists further note the irony that while lower-class women have broad access to contraceptive coverage, they have limited access to infertility treatments. Today it is possible to know the sex of the unborn. Beginning in 1998, at a cost of about $2,500, couples could purchase the expertise that would sort the sperm that is more likely to produce a baby of a desired sex. Feminist theorists are watching these developments closely. They are concerned that in societies where men enjoy a higher status, this technology will be used to effectively reduce the presence of women. Interactionists observe that the quest for information and social support connected with reproductive technology has created new social networks. (299)

KEY TERMS

Briefly define or identify the following terms in the spaces provided below. The definitions of these terms can be found later in this chapter of the study guide.

Family	Patrilineal descent
Nuclear family	Matrilineal descent
Extended family	Patriarchy
Monogamy	Matriarchy
Serial monogamy	Egalitarian family
Polygamy	Endogamy
Polygyny	Exogamy
Polyandry	Incest taboo
Kinship	Machismo
Bilateral descent	Familism

Adoption	Cohabitation
Single-parent families	Domestic partnership

SELF-TEST

MODIFIED TRUE-FALSE QUESTIONS: If the statement below is true, write "true" in the space provided. If the statement is false, briefly correct the error.

1. By 2000, more than one-half of all households in the United States fit the nuclear family model.

2. In polygynous societies, most men have multiple spouses.

3. Kinship is totally determined by biological or marital ties.

4. Many sociologists believe that the matriarchal family has begun to replace the patriarchal family as the social norm in the United States, as more and more women become self-sufficient.

5. The functionalist perspective encourages us to examine the ways in which an institution gratifies the needs of its members and contributes to the stability of society.

6. Currently, up to 90 percent of all men and women in the United States marry at least once.

7. Endogamy is intended to reinforce the cohesiveness of the group by suggesting to the young that they should marry someone "of our own kind."

8. The number of interracial marriages between African Americans and Whites in the United States has increased more than seven times jumping from 51,000 in 1960 to 363,000 in 2000.

9. Among the poor, adult women often play a significant role in the economic support of the family.

10. Adopters must be married.

11. Approximately 10 percent of all people in the United States will marry, divorce, and then remarry.

12. Men are less likely to remarry than women because they cannot afford to make child support payments and establish a new family simultaneously.

13. The number of households in the United States engaged in cohabitation increased 48 percent between 1990 and 1998.

14. The trend toward maintaining a single lifestyle for a longer period of time is related to a fear of commitment.

15. The contemporary gay liberation movement has given an increasing number of lesbians and gay men the support to proclaim their sexual and affectional orientation.

MULTIPLE-CHOICE QUESTIONS: In each of the following, select the phrase that best completes the statement.

1. Alice, age 7, lives in a private home with her parents, her grandmother, and her aunt. Alice's family is an example of a (an)
   a. nuclear family.
   b. dysfunctional family.
   c. extended family.
   d. polygynous family.

2. Some observers, noting the high rate of divorce in the United States, have suggested that the most accurate description for the form that monogamy takes in this country is
   a. functional monogamy.
   b. communal monogamy.
   c. serial monogamy.
   d. regressive monogamy.

3. According to anthropologist George Murdock, the most common type of polygamy is
   a. polygyny.
   b. polyandry.
   c. serial polygamy.
   d. matriarchy.

4. Which system of descent is followed in the United States?
   a. matrilineal
   b. patrilineal
   c. unilateral
   d. bilateral

5. Which of the following theorists described the family as the ultimate source of social inequality because of its role in the transfer of power, property, and privilege?
   a. Friedrich Engels
   b. Talcott Parsons
   c. Margaret Mead
   d. George Murdock

6. Which of the following is not a function of the family discussed by William F. Ogburn?
   a. providing of social status
   b. reproduction
   c. economic
   d. protection

7. In the United States in 2000, domestic violence resulted in
   a. more than 3 million reports of child abuse or neglect.
   b. 2 million violent crimes committed by current or former spouses, boyfriends, or girlfriends.
   c. injuries to more than 25 percent of wives.
   d. all of the above

8. Korean immigrants to the United States obtain the funds needed to begin a business by pooling their resources through an association known as a
   a. kye.
   b. domestic partnership.
   c. kagemi.
   d. kinship.

9. Which term has been used in the popular press to refer to adult children who continue to (or return to) live at home?
   a. "boomerang generation"
   b. counterculture
   c. "Brady Bunch" cohort
   d. Generation X

10. One recent development in family life in the United States has been the extension of parenthood as adult children continue to (or return to) live at home. The reason for this is
    a. the rising divorce rate and the need for help with childcare.
    b. skyrocketing rent and real estate prices.
    c. financial difficulties.
    d. all of the above

11. Which sociological perspective emphasizes that government has a strong interest in encouraging adoption?
    a. functionalist perspective
    b. conflict perspective
    c. interactionist perspective
    d. labeling theory

12. Which of the following is a factor that has contributed to the rise of the dual income model of the family?
    a. increasing number of men with a college education
    b. increasing birthrate
    c. shift in the economy of the United States from manufacturing to service industries
    d. all of the above

13. During the 1990s the rate of African American teenage pregnancy in the United States
    a. increased dramatically.
    b. declined steadily.
    c. increased slightly.
    d. remained steady.

14. Of those in the United States who obtain a divorce, about what percent later remarry?
    a. two-thirds of divorced men
    b. three-fourths of divorced women
    c. two-thirds of divorced women
    d. 80 percent of divorced women

15. Which of the following factors is associated with the high divorce rate in the United States?
    a. the liberalization of divorce laws
    b. contemporary families have fewer children than earlier families
    c. the increase in family incomes
    d. all of the above

FILL-IN QUESTIONS: Fill in the blank spaces in the sentences below with the correct words. Where two or more words are required, there will be a corresponding number of blank spaces.

1. People in the United States see the ______________ family as the preferred form of family arrangement.

2. Anthropologist George Murdock sampled 565 societies and found that over 80 percent had some type of ______________ as their preferred form of marriage.

3. The principle of ______________ assigns people to kinship groups according to their relationship to an individual's mother or father.

4. Frequently, in patriarchal societies, the ______________ male wields the greatest power.

5. ______________ emerged among Native American tribal societies, and in nations in which men were absent for long periods of time for warfare or food gathering.

6. In the view of many sociologists, the ______________ family has begun to replace the patriarchal family as the social norm in the United States.

7. As ______________ theorists point out, the social class of couples and their children significantly influences the socialization experiences to which they are exposed, and the protection they receive.

8. Interracial unions force a society to reconsider its definitions of _____________ and _____________.

9. Although social class differences in family life are less striking than they once were, _____________ class families were found to be more authoritarian in rearing children and more inclined to use physical punishment.

10. Caring for children is a _____________ function of the family, yet the ways in which different societies assign this function to family members can vary significantly.

11. Sociologist Alice Rossi points out that there is little _____________ socialization in the United States for the social roles of caregiver.

12. Although _____________ percent of single parents in the United States are mothers, the number of households headed by single fathers has more than _____________ over the period 1980 to 2000.

13. Viewed from a (an) _____________ perspective, having a child may provide a sense of motivation and purpose for a low-income teenager whose economic worth in our society is limited at best.

14. The rising rates of divorce and remarriage in the United States have led to a noticeable increase in _____________ relationships.

15. Even though the most passionate support for _____________ _____________ legislation has come from lesbian and gay male activists, the majority of those eligible for such benefits would be cohabiting heterosexual couples.

UNDERSTANDING SOCIAL POLICY: All the following questions are based on material that appears in the social policy section on Reproductive Technology. Write a brief answer to each question in the space provided below.

1. What is the functionalist analysis of reproductive technology?

2. What is the conflict theorist's view of reproductive technology?

3. What is the interactionist's view of reproductive technology?

4. What are the policy issues that concern reproductive technology?

DEFINITIONS OF KEY TERMS

Family: A set of people related by blood, marriage (or some other agreed-upon relationship), or adoption who share the responsibility for reproducing and caring for members of society. (281)

Nuclear family: A married couple and their unmarried children living together. (281)

Extended family: A family in which relatives—such as grandparents, aunts, or uncles—live in the same home as parents and their children. (281)

Monogamy: A form of marriage in which one woman and one man are married only to each other. (282)

Serial monogamy: A form of marriage in which a person can have several spouses in his or her lifetime but only one spouse at a time. (282)

Polygamy: A form of marriage in which an individual can have several husbands or wives simultaneously. (282)

Polygyny: A form of polygamy in which a husband can have several wives at the same time. (282)

Polyandry: A form of polygamy in which a woman can have several husbands at the same time. (282)

Kinship: The state of being related to others. (283)

Bilateral descent: A kinship system in which both sides of a person's family are regarded as equally important. (283)

Patrilineal descent: A kinship system that favors the relatives of the father. (283)

Matrilineal descent: A kinship system that favors the relatives of the mother. (283)

Patriarchy: A society in which men dominate family decision making. (283)

Matriarchy: A society in which women dominate family decision making. (284)

Egalitarian family: An authority pattern in which the adult members of the family are regarded as equals. (284)

Endogamy: The restriction of mate selection to people within the same group. (287)

Exogamy: The requirement that people select mates outside certain groups. (287)

Incest taboo: The prohibition of sexual relationships between certain culturally specified relatives. (287)

Machismo: A sense of virility, personal worth, and pride in one's maleness. (290)

Familism: Pride in the extended family, expressed through the maintenance of close ties and strong obligations to kinfolk. (290)

Adoption: In a legal sense, a process that allows for the transfer of the legal rights, responsibilities, and privileges of parenthood from legal parents to new legal parents. (291)

Single-parent families: Families in which there is only one parent present to care for children. (292)

Cohabitation: The practice of living together as a male-female couple without marrying. (296)

Domestic partnership: Two unrelated adults who have chosen to share one another's lives in a relationship of mutual caring, who reside together, and who agree to be jointly responsible for their dependents, basic living expenses, and other common necessities. (298)

ANSWERS TO SELF-TEST

Modified True-False Questions

1. By 2000 only about one-third of the nation's families fit the nuclear family model. (281)
2. In polygynous societies, relatively few men actually have multiple spouses. (282)
3. Kinship is culturally learned and is not totally determined by biological or marital ties. (283)
4. Many sociologists believe the egalitarian family has begun to replace the patriarchal family as the social norm in the United States. (284)
5. True (284)
6. True (286)
7. True (287)
8. True (288)
9. True (289)
10. In some cases adopters are not married and are not required to be married. (292)
11. Approximately 45 percent of all people in the United States will marry, divorce, and then remarry. (294)
12. Women are less likely to remarry than men because they most often retain custody of children after a divorce, which complicates establishing a new adult relationship. (295)
13. True (296)
14. The trend toward maintaining a single lifestyle for a longer period of time is related to the growing economic independence of young people. (297)
15. True (298)

Multiple-Choice Questions

1. c (281)
2. c (282)
3. a (282)
4. d (283)
5. a (284)
6. c (284)
7. a (285)
8. a (290)
9. a (291)
10. d (291)
11. a (291)
12. c (292)
13. b (293)
14. c (295)
15. d (295)

Fill-In Questions

1. nuclear (281)
2. polygamy (282)
3. descent (283)
4. eldest (283)
5. Matriarchies (284)
6. egalitarian (284)
7. conflict (285)
8. race and ethnicity (288)
9. lower (289)
10. universal (290)
11. anticipatory (291)
12. 82; quadrupled (293)
13. interactionist (293)
14. stepfamily (294)
15. domestic partnership (299)

Understanding Social Policy: Reproductive Technology

1. Replacing personnel is a functional prerequisite that the family as a social institution performs. Advances in reproductive technology allow childless couples to fulfill their personal and societal goals. (300)
2. The conflict perspective would note that in the world today the available technologies are often only accessible to the most affluent. Conflict theorists further note that while lower-class women have broad access to contraceptive coverage, they have limited access to infertility treatment. (300)
3. Interactionists observe that the quest for information and social support connected with reproductive technology has created new social networks. For example, Internet support groups allow couples to share their successes and their fears as they come to terms with the new reproductive technology. (300)
4. In Japan, some infertile couples have caused a controversy by using eggs or sperm donated by siblings for in vitro fertilization. Many nations, including England and Australia, bar payments to egg donors, resulting in very few donors in these countries. The legal and ethical issues connected with reproductive technology are immense. Many people feel we should be preparing for the possibility of a human clone. Already, reputable hospitals are mixing donated sperm and egg to create embryos that are frozen for future use. This raises the possibility of genetic screening as couples choose what they regard as the most "desirable" embryo, in effect, a "designer baby." (301)

CHAPTER

13 RELIGION AND EDUCATION

KEY POINTS

Émile Durkheim: Émile Durkheim was perhaps the first sociologist to recognize the critical importance of religion in human societies. He saw its appeal for the individual, but more importantly, he stressed the social impact of religion. In Durkheim's view, religion is a collective act and includes many forms of behavior in which people interact with others. Durkheim defined religion as a "unified system of beliefs and practices relative to sacred things." (307)

The Integrative Function of Religion: Émile Durkheim viewed religion as an integrative power in human society, a perspective reflected in functionalist thought today. Religion gives people certain ultimate values and ends to hold in common. The integrative function of religion is particularly apparent in traditional, pre-industrial societies. In some instances, however, religious loyalties are dysfunctional; they contribute to tension and even conflict between groups or nations. (313)

Religion and Social Support: Through its emphasis on the divine and supernatural, religion allows us to "do something about the calamities we face." Religion encourages us to view our personal misfortunes as relatively unimportant in the broader perspective of human history, or even as part of an undisclosed divine purpose. This perspective may be much more comforting than the terrifying feeling that any of us can die senselessly at any moment, and that there is no divine "answer" as to why one person lives a long and full life, whereas another dies tragically at a relatively early age. (315)

Religion and Social Change—the Weberian Thesis: Max Weber carefully examined the connection between religious allegiance and capitalist development in his pioneering work, *The Protestant Ethic and the Spirit of Capitalism.* Weber pointed out that the followers of John Calvin, a leader of the Protestant Reformation, emphasized a disciplined work ethic, this-worldly concerns, and a rational orientation to life that has become known as the Protestant ethic. Like Durkheim, Weber demonstrated that religion is not solely a matter of intimate personal beliefs. He stressed that the collective nature of religion has social consequences for society as a whole. (315)

Religion and Social Control—a Conflict View: For Karl Marx, the relationship between religion and social change was clear: religion impeded social change by encouraging oppressed people to focus on otherworldly concerns rather than on their immediate poverty or exploitation. He felt that religion often drugged the masses into submission by offering a consolation for their harsh lives on earth: the hope of salvation in an ideal afterlife. Marxists suggest that by inducing a "false consciousness" among the disadvantaged, religion lessens the possibility of collective political action that can end capitalist oppression and transform society. (316)

Religious Behavior: Religious beliefs, religious rituals, and religious experience all help to define what is sacred, and to differentiate the sacred from the profane. Religious beliefs are statements to which members of a particular religion adhere. Religious rituals are practices required or expected of members of a faith. The term **religious experience** refers to the feeling or perception of being in direct contact with the ultimate reality, such as a divine being, or of being overcome with religious emotion. (317)

Religious Organization: Sociologists find it useful to distinguish between four basic forms of organization. An **ecclesia** is a religious organization that claims to include most or all of the members of a society and is recognized as the national or official religion. A **denomination** is a large, organized religion not officially linked with the state or government. A **sect** can be defined as a relatively small religious group that has broken away from some other religious organization to renew what it considers the original vision of the faith. A **new religious movement** or **cult** is a generally small, secretive religious group that represents either a new religion or a major innovation of an existing faith. (319)

Education—Transmitting Culture: As a social institution, education performs a rather conservative function—transmitting the dominant culture. Schooling exposes each generation of young people to the existing beliefs, norms, and values of their culture. In our society we learn respect for social control and reverence for established institutions such as religion, the family, and the presidency. (323)

Promoting Social and Political Integration: Education serves the latent function of promoting social and political integration by transforming a population composed of diverse racial, ethnic, and religious groups into a society whose members share to some extent a common identity. From a functionalist perspective, the common identity and social integration fostered by education contributes to societal stability and consensus. In the past, the integrative function of education was most obvious through its emphasis on promoting a common language. (324)

Maintaining Social Control: Schools serve as a transitional agent of social control—between parents and employers in the life cycle of most individuals. Schools direct and even restrict students' aspirations in a manner that reflects societal values and prejudices. Socialization into traditional gender roles can be viewed as a form of social control. (325)

Conflict View of Schooling: Sociologist Christopher Hurn has compared the functionalist and conflict views of schooling. According to Hurn, the functionalist perspective portrays contemporary education as basically benign. For example, it argues that schools rationally sort and select students for future high-status positions, thereby meeting society's need for talented and expert personnel. By contrast, the conflict perspective views education as an instrument of elite domination. Schools convince subordinate groups of their inferiority, reinforce existing social class inequality, and discourage alternative and more democratic visions of society. (326)

Bestowal of Status: Conflict sociologists stress that schools sort pupils according to social class background. Although the educational system helps certain poor children to move into middle-class professional positions, it denies most disadvantaged children the same educational opportunities afforded children of the affluent. In this way, schools tend to preserve social class inequalities in each new generation. Even a single school can reinforce class differences by putting students in tracks. Thus, working-class children, assumed to be destined for subordinate positions, are more likely to be placed in high school vocational and general tracks, which emphasize close supervision and compliance with authority. (327)

Treatment of Women in Education: In the twentieth century, sexism in education existed in many ways: in textbooks with negative stereotypes of women, counselors' pressure on female students to prepare for "women's work," and unequal funding for women's and men's athletic programs. But perhaps nowhere has educational discrimination been more evident than in the employment of teachers. Men generally fill the positions of university professor and college administrator, and both positions hold relatively high status in the United States. (328)

Education—the Interactionist View: The labeling approach and the concept of the self-fulfilling prophecy suggest that if we treat people in particular ways, they may fulfill our expectations. A dominant group's stereotyping of racial minorities may limit their opportunities to break away from expected roles. Studies in the United States have revealed that teachers wait longer for an answer from a student believed to be a high achiever, and they are more likely to give such children a second chance. (329)

Schools as Formal Organizations: Max Weber noted five basic characteristics of bureaucracy, all of which are evident in the vast majority of schools. (1) A division of labor: specialized experts teach particular age levels of students and specific subjects. (2) A hierarchy of authority: each employee of a school system is responsible to a higher authority. (3) Written rules and regulations: Teachers and administrators must conform to numerous rules and regulations in the performance of their duties. (4) Impersonality: the university has been portrayed as a giant, face-less bureaucracy that cares little for the uniqueness of the individual. (5) Employment based on technical qualifications: At least in theory, the hiring of teachers and college professors is based on professional competence and expertise. (330)

Religion in the Schools: The government is required to protect the right to practice one's religion, but on the other hand, it cannot take any measures that would seem to "establish" one religion over another (the church/state separation). In the key case of *Engle v. Vitale*, the Supreme Court ruled in 1962 that the use of nondenominational prayer in New York schools was "wholly inconsistent" with the First Amendment's prohibition against government establishment of religion. In the "monkey trial" of 1925 a high school biology teacher, John T. Scopes, was convicted of violating a Tennessee law making it a crime to teach the scientific theory of evolution in schools. Viewed from a conflict perspective, organized school prayer could reinforce the religious beliefs, rituals, and interests of the powerful; violate the rights of the powerless; increase religious dissension; and threaten the cultural and religious pluralism of the United States. Drawing on the interactionist perspective and small group research, sociologists suggest that children will face enormous social pressure to conform to the beliefs and practices of a religious majority. (334)

KEY TERMS

Briefly define or identify the following terms in the spaces provided below. The definitions of these terms can be found later in this chapter of the study guide.

Cultural universals	Religious beliefs
Secularization	Religious rituals
Education	Religious experience
Religion	Ecclesia
Sacred	Denomination
Profane	Sect
Protestant ethic	Established sect
Liberation theology	New religious movement (NRM) or cult

Hidden curriculum	Correspondence principle
Credentialism	Teacher-expectancy effect
Tracking	Creationism

SELF-TEST

MODIFIED TRUE-FALSE QUESTIONS: If the statement below is true, write "true" in the space provided. If the statement is false, briefly correct the error.

1. The same object can be either sacred or profane, depending on how it is viewed.

2. Church services are a meeting ground for unmarried members. This is a manifest function of religions.

3. The "cultural war" taking place in the United States is between Christian fundamentalists, conservative Catholics, and Orthodox Jews.

4. In Max Weber's *The Protestant Ethic and the Spirit of Capitalism*, he noted that in European nations with both Jewish and Protestant citizens, an overwhelming number of business leaders, owners of capital, and skilled workers were Jewish.

5. Karl Marx argued that religion impeded social change by encouraging oppressed people to focus on other-worldly concerns rather than on their immediate poverty or exploitation.

6. Sects are often short-lived, but those that are able to survive may, over time, become less antagonistic and begin to resemble denominations.

7. Through the exercise of social control, schools teach students various skills and values essential to their future positions within the labor force. They learn punctuality, discipline, scheduling, and responsible work habits, as well as how to negotiate their way through the complexities of a bureaucratic organization.

8. Numerous sociological studies have revealed that increased years of formal schooling are associated with openness to new ideas and more liberal social and political viewpoints.

9. The hidden curriculum is a unique characteristic of schools in the United States, which is fostered by the bureaucratic structure of that institution.

10. In the view of conflict theorists, the educational inequalities resulting from tracking are designed to meet the needs of modern capitalist society.

11. It has been estimated that about 2 percent of elementary schools in the United States, and 3 percent of secondary schools, use some form of tracking.

12. According to the correspondence principle, schools with students from different social classes promote the values of the White middle class to further the process of cultural assimilation.

13. The labeling approach and the concept of the self-fulfilling prophecy suggest that if we treat people in a particular way, they may fulfill our expectations.

14. Schools provide for students' social and recreational needs, thereby fulfilling a manifest function of education.

15. As a result of the rise in school violence, children are safer in their neighborhoods than they are in their schools.

MULTIPLE-CHOICE QUESTIONS: In each of the following, select the phrase that best completes the statement.

1. Which of the following sociologists stressed the social impact of religion, and was perhaps the first to recognize the critical importance of religion in human societies?
   a. Max Weber
   b. Émile Durkheim
   c. Karl Marx
   d. Talcott Parsons

2. Which sociological perspective emphasizes the integrative power of religion in human society?
   a. functionalist perspective
   b. conflict perspective
   c. interactionist perspective
   d. all of the above

3. Religion defines the spiritual world and gives meaning to the divine. These are _______________ functions of religion.
   a. manifest
   b. latent
   c. positive
   d. negative

4. One by-product of Max Weber's pioneering work, *The Protestant Ethic and the Spirit of Capitalism* was
   a. a drive to accumulate savings.
   b. to serve God without pursuit of tangible items.
   c. a recognition that "God's will" will be understood another time.
   d. none of the above

5. Liberation theology is the use of the Roman Catholic church in a political effort to eliminate poverty, discrimination, and other forms of injustice in
   a. Europe.
   b. East Africa.
   c. Latin America.
   d. Southeast Asia.

6. Which sociological perspective argues that to whatever extent religion actually does influence social behavior, it reinforces existing patterns of dominance and inequality?
   a. functionalist perspective
   b. conflict perspective
   c. interactionist perspective
   d. all of the above

7. By far the largest single denomination in the United States is
   a. Lutheranism.
   b. Episcopalianism.
   c. Southern Baptist.
   d. Roman Catholicism.

8. Which one of the following is a manifest function of education?
   a. bestowing status
   b. transmitting culture
   c. promoting social and political change
   d. all of the above

9. Which one of the following was introduced into school systems to promote social change?
   a. sex education classes
   b. affirmative action programs
   c. Project Head Start
   d. all of the above

10. The trend toward credentialism was anticipated as far back as 1916 by
    a. Émile Durkheim.
    b. Max Weber.
    c. Karl Marx.
    d. Charles Horton Cooley.

11. Which sociological perspective emphasizes that the widening bestowal of status granted by the educational system is beneficial not only to particular recipients but to the society as a whole?
    a. the functionalist perspective
    b. the conflict perspective
    c. the interactionist perspective
    d. the labeling approach

12. Which perspective contends that schools tend to preserve social class inequalities in each new generation?
    a. the functionalist perspective
    b. the conflict perspective
    c. the interactionist perspective
    d. anomie theory

13. The teacher-expectancy effect is most closely associated with the
    a. functionalist perspective.
    b. conflict perspective.
    c. interactionist perspective.
    d. anomie theory.

14. Which of the following statements about school violence is true?
    a. A child has only a one in 1,000 chance of being killed at school.
    b. The number of people shot and killed in school in the 1998-1999 school year was 400, about average over the last two decades.
    c. According to the Center for Disease Control, 47 percent of violent deaths of school-aged children in 1996-1999 occurred outside school grounds.
    d. Fewer students are now being found with guns in school.

15. The student subculture that is hostile to the college environment and seeks out ideas that may or may not relate to studies is called the
    a. collegiate subculture.
    b. academic subculture.
    c. vocational subculture.
    d. nonconformist subculture.

FILL-IN QUESTIONS: Fill in the blank spaces in the sentences below with the correct words. Where two or more words are required, there will be a corresponding number of blank spaces.

1. The _____________ encompasses elements beyond everyday life that inspire awe, respect, and even fear as compared to the _____________, which includes the ordinary and commonplace.

2. _____________ theorists caution that Weber's theory of the Protestant ethic, even if it is accepted, should not be regarded as an analysis of mature capitalism as reflected in the rise of large corporations that transcend national boundaries.

3. Weber pointed out that followers of John Calvin, a leader of the Protestant Reformation, emphasized a disciplined work ethic, this-worldly concerns, and a rational orientation to life that have become known as the _____________ _____________.

4. A possible dysfunction of _____________ _____________ would be the belief that when Roman Catholics focus on political and governmental injustice, the clergy are no longer addressing their personal and spiritual needs.

5. _____________ _____________ are statements to which members of a particular religion adhere.

6. Unlike ecclesiae and denominations, _____________ require intensive commitments and demonstrations of belief by members.

7. Schools provide a variety of _____________ functions, such as the transmitting of culture, promoting social and political integration, and maintaining social control.

8. In the past, the integrative function of education was most obvious through its emphasis on promoting a common _____________.

9. According to the _____________ curriculum, children must not speak until the teacher calls on them, and must regulate their activities according to the clock or bell.

10. In the twentieth century, _____________ in education has been manifested in many ways: in textbooks with negative stereotypes of women, counselors' pressure on female students to prepare for "women's work," and unequal funding for women and men's recreational programs.

11. The _____________ of schools in the United States has resulted not only from the growing number of students being served by individual schools and school systems, but also from the greater degree of specialization required within a technologically complex society.

12. The bureaucratic characteristic of written rules and regulations can become _____________ in schools, since the time invested in completing required forms could instead be spent in preparing lessons or conferring with students.

13. The _____________ subculture identifies with the intellectual concerns of the faculty and values knowledge for its own sake.

14. The "big bang" theory is challenged by _____________ who hold to the biblical account of the creation of humans and the universe.

15. The issue of religion in our schools goes to the heart of the _____________ Amendment provisions on religious freedoms. The government is required to protect the right to practice one's religion, but it cannot take any measure that would seem to "establish" one religion over another: this is known as the _____________/_____________ _____________.

UNDERSTANDING SOCIAL POLICY: All the following questions are based on material that appears in the social policy section on Religion in the Schools. Write a brief answer to each question in the space provided below.

1. What is creationism and why is it a social issue in the United States?

2. What is the "monkey trial"?

3. What is the view of conflict theorists about school prayer?

4. What actions have been taken in Kansas, New Mexico, and Alabama concerning creationism?

DEFINITIONS OF KEY TERMS

Cultural universals: General practices found in every culture. (307)

Secularization: The process through which religion's influence on other social institutions diminishes. (307)

Education: A formal process of learning in which some people consciously teach while others adopt the social role of learner. (307)

Religion: A unified system of beliefs and practices relative to sacred things. (307)

Sacred: Elements beyond everyday life that inspire awe, respect, and even fear. (309)

Profane: The ordinary and commonplace elements of life, as distinguished from the sacred. (309)

Protestant ethic: Max Weber's term for the disciplined work ethic, this-worldly concerns, and rational orientation to life emphasized by John Calvin and his followers. (315)

Liberation theology: Use of a church, primarily Roman Catholicism, in a political effort to eliminate poverty, discrimination, and other forms of injustice evident in secular society. (315)

Religious beliefs: Statements to which members of a particular religion adhere. (317)

Religious rituals: Practices required or expected of members of a faith. (318)

Religious experience: The feeling or perception of being in direct contact with the ultimate reality, such as a divine being, or of being overcome with religious emotion. (319)

Ecclesia: A religious organization that claims to include most or all of the members of a society and is recognized as the national or official religion. (320)

Denomination: A large, organized religion not officially linked with the state or government. (320)

Sect: A relatively small religious group that has broken away from some other religious organization to renew what it views as the original vision of the faith. (320)

Established sect: A religious group that is the outgrowth of a sect, yet remains isolated from society. (320)

New Religious Movement (NRM) or cult: A generally small, secretive religious group that represents either a new religion or a major innovation of an existing faith. (321)

Hidden curriculum: Standards of behavior that are deemed proper by society and are taught subtly in school. (326)

Credentialism: An increase in the lowest level of education required to enter a field. (327)

Tracking: The practice of placing students in specific curriculum groups on the basis of test scores and other criteria. (327)

Correspondence principle: The tendency of schools to promote the values expected of individuals in each social class and to prepare students for the types of jobs typically held by members of their class. (328)

Teacher-expectancy effect: The impact that a teacher's expectations about a student's performance may have on the student's actual achievements. (329)

Creationism: A literal interpretation of the Bible regarding the creation of humanity and the universe used to argue that evolution should not be presented as established scientific fact. (334)

ANSWERS TO SELF-TEST

Modified True-False Questions

1. True (309)
2. Church services are a meeting ground for unmarried members. This is a latent function of religions. (313)
3. The "cultural war" refers to Christian fundamentalists, conservative Catholics, and Orthodox Jews joining forces in many communities to battle against their liberal counterparts for control of the secular culture. (314)
4. In Max Weber's *The Protestant Ethic and the Spirit of Capitalism*, he noted that in European nations with both Catholic and Protestant citizens, an overwhelming number of business leaders, owners of capital, and skilled workers were Protestants. (315)
5. True (316)
6. True (320)
7. True (325)
8. True (326)
9. A hidden curriculum is evident in schools around the world. (326)
10. True (328)
11. It has been estimated that about 60 percent of elementary schools in the United States, and 80 percent of secondary schools, use some form of tracking. (328)
12. According to the correspondence principle, schools with students from different social classes promote the values expected of individuals in each class, and perpetuate social class divisions from one generation to the next. (328)
13. True (329)
14. Schools provide for students' social and recreational needs, thereby fulfilling a latent function of education. (331)
15. Schools are safer than neighborhoods for children. (332)

Multiple Choice Questions

1. b (307)
2. a (313)
3. a (313)
4. a (315)
5. c (315)
6. b (317)
7. d (320)
8. a (323)
9. d (325)
10. b (327)
11. a (327)
12. b (327)
13. c (329)
14. d (332)
15. d (334)

Fill-In Questions

1. sacred; profane (309)
2. Conflict (315)
3. Protestant ethic (315)
4. liberation theology (316)
5. Religious beliefs (317)
6. sects (320)
7. latent (323)
8. language (325)
9. hidden (326)
10. sexism (328)
11. bureaucratization (330)
12. dysfunctional (330)
13. academic (334)
14. creationists (334)
15. First; church/state separation (334)

Understanding Social Policy: Religion in the Schools

1. Creationism is a literal interpretation of the bible regarding the creation of man and the universe used to argue that evolution should not be presented as established scientific fact. Creationists want their theory taught in schools as the only one, or at the very least, as an alternative to the theory of evolution. (334)
2. The controversy over whether the biblical account of creation should be presented in school curricula recalls the famous "monkey trial" of 1925. In this trial, high school biology teacher John T. Scopes was convicted of violating a Tennessee law making it a crime to teach the scientific theory of evolution in public schools. (335)
3. Opponents of school prayer and creationism argue that a religious majority in a community might impose religious viewpoints specific to its faith, at the expense of religious minorities. Viewed from a conflict perspective, organized school prayer could reinforce the religious beliefs, rituals, and interests of the powerful, violate the rights of the powerless, increase religious dissension, and threaten the culture and religious pluralism of the United States. These critics question whether school prayer can remain truly voluntary. (335)
4. In 1999 the Kansas Board of Education caused a stir when it voted to delete from the state's science curriculum virtually any mention of evolution, and to remove from standardized tests questions having to do with the theory of evolution or the "big bang" theory of the creation of the universe. Later, when the composition of the board changed, the controversial decision was overturned. (335)

CHAPTER

14 GOVERNMENT, THE ECONOMY, AND THE ENVIRONMENT

KEY POINTS

The Political System: By **political system**, sociologists mean the social institution that is founded on a recognized set of procedures for implementing and achieving society's goals. Like religion and the family, the political system is a cultural universal; it is found in every society. (341)

The Economic System: The term **economic system** refers to the social institution through which goods and services are produced, distributed, and consumed. As with social institutions—such as the family, religion, and government—the economic system shapes other aspects of the social order, and is in turn, influenced by them. (341)

Capitalism: Capitalism is an economic system in which the means of production are largely in private hands and the main incentive for economic activity is the accumulation of profit. In practice, capitalist systems vary in the degree to which the government regulates private ownership and economic activity. Contemporary capitalism features government regulation of economic relations and tolerance of monopolistic practices. The principle of free competition has been seriously compromised in contemporary capitalist societies. (342)

Socialism: Socialist theory was refined in the writings of Karl Marx and Friedrich Engels. Under socialism, the means of production and distribution in a society are collectively, rather than privately owned. The basic objective of the economic system is to meet people's needs rather than to maximize profits. In theory, the wealth of the people as a collectivity is used to provide health care, housing, education, and other key services for each individual and family. Marx believed that each socialist state would eventually "wither away" and evolve into a communist state. As an ideal type, communism refers to an economic system under which all property is communally owned and no social distinctions are made on the basis of people's ability to produce. (343)

Power: Power is at the heart of a political system. Max Weber defined **power** as the ability to exercise one's will over others. Power relations can involve large organizations, small groups, or even people in an intimate association, such as a family. There are three basic sources of power within any political system: force, influence, and authority. (344)

Types of Authority: Max Weber identified three ideal types of authority. In a political system based on **traditional authority**, legitimate power is conferred by custom and accepted practice. Authority does not rest in personal characteristics, technical competence, or even written law. Power made legitimate by law is known as **legal-rational authority**. Leaders of such societies derive their authority from the written rules and regulations of political systems. The term **charismatic authority** refers to power made legitimate by a leader's exceptional personal or emotional appeal to his or her followers. Charisma allows a person to lead or inspire without relying on set rules or traditions. (345)

Political Socialization: Political socialization is the process by which individuals acquire political attitudes and develop patterns of political behavior. In the view of conflict theorists, students in the United States learn much more than factual information about their political and economic way of life. They are socialized to view capitalism and representative democracy as the "normal" and most desirable ways of organizing a nation, a form of dominant ideology. The principal institutions of political socialization are those that also socialize us to other cultural norms, including the family, schools, and the media. (348)

Women in Politics: Women continue to be dramatically underrepresented in the halls of government. As of early 2002, there were only 73 women in Congress. They accounted for 60 of the 435 members of the House of Representatives and 13 of the 100 members of the Senate. Only five states had female governors: Arizona, Delaware, Massachusetts, Montana and New Hampshire. A new dimension of women and politics emerged beginning in the 1980s. Surveys detected a growing "gender gap" in the political preferences and activities of males and females. (350)

Elite and Pluralist Models of Power Relations: Who really holds power in the United States? Like others who hold an elite model of power relations, Karl Marx believed that society is ruled by a small group of individuals who share a common set of political and economic interests. Sociologist C. Wright Mills argued that power rested in the hands of a few, both inside and outside government—the **power elite**. Sociologist G. William Domhoff stresses the role played both by elites of the corporate community and by the leaders of policy-formation organizations, such as chambers of commerce and labor unions. Critics of the elite model of power relations insist that power is more widely shared than Marx, Mills, and Domhoff indicate. In their view, a **pluralist model** more accurately describes the nation's political system. In a pluralist model, many conflicting groups within the community have access to government so that no single group is dominant. (350)

The Face of the Workforce: The number of Black, Latino, and Asian American workers continues to increase at a rate faster than the number of White workers. More and more, the workforce reflects the diversity of the population, as ethnic minorities enter the labor force, and as immigrants and their children move from marginal jobs or employment in the informal economy to positions of greater visibility and responsibility. Interactionists note that people will find themselves supervising and being supervised by people very different from themselves. (353)

Deindustrialization and Downsizing: The term **deindustrialization** refers to the systematic, widespread withdrawal of investment in basic aspects of productivity, such as factories and plants. Some companies relocate from northeastern and midwestern states to southern states, while others relocate outside the United States to countries with lower rates of prevailing wages. The term **downsizing** was introduced in 1987 to refer to reductions in a company's work force. Viewed from a conflict perspective, the unprecedented attention given to downsizing in the mid-1990s reflected the continuing importance of social class in the United States. Conflict theorists note that job loss, affecting factory workers in particular, has long been a feature of industrialization. But when large numbers of middle-class managers and other white-collar employees with substantial incomes began to be laid off, suddenly there was great concern in the media over downsizing. (354)

Environmental Problems—an Overview: More than 1 billion people on the planet are exposed to potentially health-damaging levels of air pollution. Throughout the United States, streams, rivers, and lakes have been polluted by dumping of waste materials by both industries and local governments. Love Canal made it clear that land can be seriously contaminated by industrial dumping of hazardous wastes and chemicals. Neo-Malthusians such as Paul Ehrlich and Anne Ehrlich see world population growth as the central factor in environmental deterioration. Barry Commoner, a biologist, counters that the primary cause of environmental ills is the increasing use of technological innovations that are destructive to the world's environment. Allan Schnaiberg, a sociologist, argues that those who own and control the means of production in advanced capitalist societies have ultimate responsibility for our environmental problems because of their need to constantly generate greater profits no matter what the environmental consequences. (356)

Functionalism and Human Ecology: In an application of the human ecological perspective, sociologist Riley Dunlap suggests that the natural environment serves three basic purposes for humans, as it does for the many animal species: (1) the environment provides the resources essential for life; (2) the environment serves as a waste repository; and (3) the environment "houses" our species. Human use of the environment for one of these functions will often strain its ability to fulfill the other two. (358)

Conflict View of Environmental Issues: World systems analysis shows how a growing share of the human and natural resources of the developing countries is being redistributed to the core industrialized nations. This process only intensifies the destruction of natural resources in poorer regions of the world. From a conflict perspective, less affluent nations are being forced to exploit their mineral deposits, forests, and fisheries in order to meet their debt obligations. (359)

Affirmative Action: The term affirmative action refers to positive efforts to recruit minority group members or women for jobs, promotions, and educational opportunities. But many people feel that affirmative action programs constitute reverse discrimination of qualified Whites and males. Conflict theorists view affirmative action as a legislative attempt to reduce inequality embedded in the social structure by increasing opportunities to groups such as women and African Americans. Interactionists focus on situations in which some women and minorities in underrepresented professions and schools are often mistakenly viewed as products of affirmative action. There is evidence that the move against affirmative action may not be as dramatic as originally thought. (360)

KEY TERMS

Briefly define or identify the following terms in the spaces provided below. The definitions of these terms can be found later in this chapter of the study guide.

Political system	Politics
Economic system	Power
Industrial society	Force
Capitalism	Influence
Laissez-faire	Authority
Monopoly	Terrorism
Socialism	Traditional authority
Communism	Legal-rational authority
Informal economy	Charismatic authority

Political socialization	Downsizing
Elite model	E-commerce
Power elite	Human ecology
Pluralist model	Environmental justice
Deindustrialization	Affirmative action

SELF-TEST

MODIFIED TRUE-FALSE QUESTIONS: If the statement below is true, write "true" in the space provided. If the statement is false, briefly correct the error.

1. Monopolistic practices are a key component of laissez-faire capitalism as it was explained by British economist Adam Smith.

2. Government ownership of all major industries, including steel production, automobile manufacturing, and agriculture, is a major feature of socialism as an ideal type.

3. In Marx's view, communist societies will naturally "wither away" and evolve out of the stage of capitalism.

4. In reality, the economy of each industrial society—the United States, Great Britain, and Japan—includes elements of both capitalism and socialism.

5. There are four basic sources of power within any political system: force, influence, coercion, and authority.

6. Max Weber developed a classification system regarding authority in which he distinguished between rational, traditional-legal, and charismatic.

7. Generally, in societies based on legal-rational authority, leaders are viewed as having absolute power passed down from generation to generation.

8. With respect to the "gender gap," in political preferences women are more likely to register as Democrats than as Republicans.

9. Karl Marx believed that society is ruled by a small group of individuals who share a common set of political and economic interests.

10. Sociologist G. William Domhoff argued that the United States is controlled by a powerful elite, that is largely white, male and upper class.

11. Deindustrialization occurs when giant corporations refuse to invest in new economic opportunities.

12. Viewed from a functionalist perspective, the unprecedented attention given to downsizing in the mid-1990s reflected the continuing importance of social class in the United States.

13. On the societal, or macro, level, the impact of a plant closing is not nearly as difficult on the community as it is on the individual worker.

14. Today the use of the contingent workforce is primarily in low-skill positions, such as fast-food restaurants.

15. Urban ecologists point out that western industrialized nations account for only 25 percent of the world's population, but are responsible for 85 percent of worldwide consumption.

MULTIPLE CHOICE QUESTIONS: In each of the following, select the phrase that best completes the statement.

1. Which two basic types of economic systems distinguish contemporary industrial societies?
   a. capitalism and communism
   b. capitalism and socialism
   c. socialism and communism
   d. capitalism and dictatorships

2. Which sociological perspective points out that while pure monopolies are not a basic element of the economy of the United States, competition is much more restricted than one might expect in what is called a free enterprise system?
   a. the functionalist perspective
   b. the conflict perspective
   c. the interactionist perspective
   d. labeling theory

3. There are three basic sources of power within any political system:
   a. force, influence, and authority.
   b. force, influence, and democracy.
   c. force, legitimacy, and charisma.
   d. influence, charisma, and bureaucracy.

4. Which of the following is not part of the classification system of authority that was developed by Max Weber?
   a. traditional authority
   b. pluralist authority
   c. legal-rational authority
   d. charismatic authority

5. A king or queen is accepted as ruler of a nation simply by virtue of inheriting the crown. This is an example of
   a. totalitarianism.
   b. charismatic authority.
   c. traditional authority.
   d. legal-rational authority.

6. The authority of the president of the United States and the Congress is legitimized by the Constitution. This is an example of
   a. political efficacy.
   b. charismatic authority.
   c. traditional authority.
   d. legal-rational authority.

7. Which of the following can be classified as a charismatic leader?
   a. Joan of Arc
   b. Malcolm X
   c. Adolf Hitler
   d. all of the above

8. Totalitarian societies commonly use ____________ institutions to indoctrinate students in political beliefs because that institution is susceptible to centralized and uniform control.
   a. family
   b. economic
   c. religious
   d. educational

9. In C. Wright Mills's power elite framework, which one of the following is not at the top of the power structure in the United States?
   a. the corporate rich
   b. leaders of the executive branch of government
   c. heads of the military
   d. members of the Supreme Court and legislative leaders

10. Sociologists and labor specialists foresee a workforce increasingly composed of
    a. women.
    b. Racial minorities.
    c. Ethnic minorities.
    d. All of the above

11. The systematic, widespread withdrawal of investment of basic aspects of productivity such as factories and plants is called
    a. de-industrialization.
    b. downsizing.
    c. postindustrialization.
    d. "banana time."

12. According to the United States Department of Labor, about ____________ percent of "downsized" employees find new jobs.
    a. 75
    b. 14
    c. 19
    d. 28

13. According to Riley Dunlop, which one of the following is not a basic function that the natural environment serves for humans?
    a. It provides the resources essential for life.
    b. It serves as a waste depository.
    c. It provides a natural setting for social inequalities.
    d. It "houses" our species.

14. Conflict theorists contend that blaming developing countries for the world's environmental deterioration contains an element of
    a. ethnocentrism.
    b. xenocentrism.
    c. separatism.
    d. goal displacement.

15. In 1978, in the _____________ case, the United States Supreme Court ruled that it was unconstitutional to have a fixed quota system for minority students, but that it was constitutional for universities to adopt flexible admissions programs that use race as one factor in decision making.
    a. Brown
    b. Bakke
    c. Roe
    d. Weber

FILL-IN QUESTIONS: Fill in the blank spaces in the sentences below with the correct words. Where two or more words are required, there will be a corresponding number of blank spaces.

1. Like religion and the family, the political system is a _____________ _____________; it is a social institution found in every society.

2. Under _____________ as an ideal type, government rarely takes over ownership of an entire industry.

3. Some capitalist nations, such as the United States, outlaw _____________ through anti-trust legislation.

4. _____________ is an economic system under which all property is communally owned and no social distinctions are made on the basis of people's ability to produce.

5. Capitalism and socialism serve as ____________ ____________ of economic systems; the economy of each industrial society includes certain elements of both these types of economic systems.

6. ____________ is the use or threat of violence against random or symbolic targets in pursuit of political aims.

7. Joan of Arc, Mahatama Gandhi, Malcolm X, and Martin Luther King are all examples of ____________ leaders.

8. The process by which you acquire political attitudes and develop patterns of political behavior is known as ____________ ____________.

9. ____________ has been the most serious barrier to women interested in holding office.

10. A new dimension of women and politics emerged beginning in the 1980s. Surveys detected a growing "____________ ____________" in the political preferences and activities of males and females. Women were more likely than men to register as Democrats than as Republicans.

11. Advocates of the ____________ model suggest that conflicting groups within the community have access to government so that no single group is dominant.

12. ____________ refers to the numerous ways that people with access to the Internet can do business from their computer.

13. In association with the deindustrialization and downsizing of industry, a "____________ work force," in which workers are hired only for as long as they are needed, has emerged in the United States.

14. In an application of the ____________ ____________ perspective, one sociologist suggests that the natural environment serves three basic functions for humans and for many animal species.

15. In respect to affirmative action, the "Q word" was ____________.

UNDERSTANDING SOCIAL POLICY: All the following questions are based on material that appears in the social policy section on Affirmative Action. Write a brief answer to each question in the space provided below.

1. What forms of job description based on race, sex, or both have been outlawed by court decisions, and by executive branch statements?

2. What is the conflict view of affirmative action?

3. According to surveys, how do the people of the United States feel about affirmative action?

DEFINITIONS OF KEY TERMS

Political system: The social institution that relies on a recognized set of procedures for implementing and achieving the goals of a group. (341)

Economic system: The social institution through which goods and services are produced, distributed, and consumed. (341)

Industrial society: A society that depends on mechanization to produce its goods and ser-vices. (341)

Capitalism: An economic system in which the means of production are largely in private hands, and the main incentive for economic activity is the accumulation of profits. (342)

Laissez-faire: A form of capitalism under which people compete freely, with minimal government intervention in the economy. (342)

Monopoly: Control of a market by a single business firm. (342)

Socialism: An economic system under which the means of production and distribution are collectively owned. (343)

Communism: As an ideal type, an economic system under which all property is communally owned and no social distinctions are made on the basis of people's ability to produce. (343)

Informal economy: Transfers of money, goods, or services that are not reported to the government (344)

Politics: In Harold D. Lasswell's words, "who gets what, when, and how." (344)

Power: The ability to exercise one's will over others. (344)

Force: The actual or threatened use of coercion to impose one's will on others. (344)

Influence: The exercise of power through a process of persuasion. (344)

Authority: Power that has been institutionalized and is recognized by the people over whom it is exercised. (345)

Terrorism: The use or threat of violence against random or symbolic targets in pursuit of political aims. (346)

Traditional authority: Legitimate power conferred by custom and accepted practice. (346)

Legal-rational authority: Power made legitimate by law. (346)

Charismatic authority: Power made legitimate by a leader's exceptional personal or emotional appeal to his or her followers. (347)

Political socialization: The process by which individuals acquire political attitudes and develop patterns of political behavior. (348)

Elite model: A view of society as ruled by a small group of individuals who share a common set of political and economic interests. (351)

Power elite: A small group of industrial, military, and government leaders who control the fate of the United States. (351)

Pluralist model: A view of society in which many competing groups have access to government so that no single group is dominant. (352)

Deindustrialization: The systematic, widespread withdrawal of investment in basic aspects of productivity such as factories. (354)

Downsizing: Reductions taken in a company's work force as part of deindustrialization. (354)

E-commerce: Numerous ways that people with access to the Internet can do business from their computer. (355)

Human ecology: An area of study concerned with the interrelationships of people and their environment. (358)

Environmental justice: A legal strategy based on claims that racial minorities are subjected disproportionately to environmental hazards. (360)

Affirmative action: Positive efforts to recruit minority group members or women for jobs, promotions, and educational opportunities. (360)

ANSWERS TO SELF-TEST

Modified True-False Questions

1. Monopolistic practices violate the ideal of free competition cherished by Adam Smith and other supporters of laissez-faire capitalism. (342)
2. True (343)
3. In Marx's view, socialist states will naturally "whiter away" and evolve into a communist society. (343)
4. True (344)
5. There are three basic sources of power within any political system: force, influence, and authority. (344)
6. Max Weber developed a classification system regarding authority in which he distinguished between traditional, legal-rational, and charismatic. (345)
7. Generally, in societies based on traditional authority, leaders are viewed as having absolute power passed down from generation to generation. (345)
8. True (350)
9. True (351)
10. True (351)
11. Deindustrialization occurs when the targets and locations of investment change, and the need for labor decreases as technology continues to automate production. (354)
12. Viewed from a conflict perspective, the unprecedented attention given to downsizing in the mid-1990s reflected the continuing importance of social class in the United States. (354)
13. On the societal, or macro, level, the impact of a plant closing on a community can be as difficult as it is for an individual worker. (355)
14. Today, the contingent workforce is evident at virtually *all* skill levels and in *all* industries. (356)
15. Conflict theorists point out that western industrialized nations account for only 25 percent of the world's population, but are responsible for 85 percent of worldwide consumption. (354)

Multiple-Choice Questions

1. b (342)
2. b (343)
3. a (344)
4. b (345)
5. c (346)
6. d (346)
7. d (347)
8. d (348)
9. d (351)
10. d (353)
11. a (354)
12. a (354)
13. c (358)
14. a (359)
15. b (361)

Fill-In Questions

1. cultural universal (341)
2. capitalism (342)
3. monopolies (343)
4. Communism (343)
5. ideal types (344)
6. Terrorism (346)
7. charismatic (347)
8. political socialization (348)
9. Sexism (350)
10. gender gap (350)
11. pluralist (352)
12. E-commerce (355)
13. contingency (355)
14. human ecological (358)
15. quota (362)

Understanding Social Policy: Affirmative Action

1. A variety of court decisions and executive branch statements have outlawed certain forms of job discrimination based on race, sex, or both, including (1) word-of-mouth recruitment among all-White or all-male work forces, (2) recruitment exclusively in schools or colleges that are limited to one sex or are predominantly White, (3) discrimination against married women or forced retirement of pregnant women, (4) advertising in male and female "help wanted" columns when gender is not a legitimate occupational qualification, and (5) job qualifications and tests that are not substantially related to the job. (361)
2. Conflict theorists view affirmative action as a legislative attempt to reduce inequality embedded in the social structure by increasing opportunities to groups, such as women and African Americans that have been deprived in the past. (361)
3. Even if they acknowledged the disparity in earnings between White males and others, many people in the United States doubt that everything done in the name of affirmative action is desirable. In a 2001 national survey, 58 percent pf respondents said they thought the approach had been good for the nation. But in response to another question, 35 percent said that affirmative action programs would be cut back; only 24 percent supported expanding them. (361)

CHAPTER 15

POPULATION, HEALTH, AND COMMUNITIES

KEY POINTS

Demography: **Demography** is the scientific study of population. It draws on several components of population—including size, composition, and territorial distribution—to understand the social consequences of population. Demographers study geographical variations and historical trends in their effort to develop population forecasts. They also analyze the structure of a population—the age, gender, race, and ethnicity of its members. (368)

Malthus's Thesis and Marx's Response: The Reverend Thomas Robert Malthus suggested that the world's population was growing more rapidly than the available food supply. Malthus saw population control as an answer to this problem, and argued that couples must take responsibility for the number of children they choose to bear. Karl Marx strongly criticized Malthus's views on population. Marx believed that capitalism, rather than rising world population, was the cause of social ills. (369)

Studying Population Today: In the United States and most other countries, the census is the primary mechanism for collecting population information. A census is an enumeration or counting of a population. The Constitution of the United States requires that a census be held every 10 years to determine congressional representation. This periodic investigation is supplemented by vital statistics; these records of births, deaths, marriages, and divorces are gathered through a registration system maintained by governmental units. (370)

Demographic Transition: Beginning in the late 1700s, and continuing until the middle 1900s, there was a gradual reduction in deathrates in northern and western Europe. While deathrates fell, birthrates remained high; as a result, there was unprecedented population growth during this period of European history. Such changes serve as an example of **demographic transition**. Specifically, demographic transition is the change from high birthrates and deathrates to relatively low birthrates and deathrates. Demographic transition should be regarded not as a "law of growth" but as a generalization of the population history of industrial nations. (371)

The Population Explosion: Apart from war, rapid population growth has been perhaps the dominant international social problem of the past 40 years. Often this issue is referred to in emotional terms, such as the "population bomb" or "population explosion." Such striking language is not surprising given the staggering increases in world population during the twentieth century. The population of our planet rose from 1 billion around the year 1800 to 6.1 billion by 2001. (373)

The Baby Boom: The most recent period of high fertility in the United States has often been referred to as the **baby boom**. During World War II, large numbers of military personnel were separated from their spouses, but when they returned, the annual number of births began to rise dramatically. The boom resulted from a striking decrease in the number of childless marriages and one-child families. Although a peak was reached in 1957, the nation maintained a relatively high birthrate of over 20 live births per 1,000 population until 1964. (374)

Stable Population Growth: In the 1980s and early 1990s, some analysts projected that there would be relatively low fertility levels and moderate net migration over the coming decades. As a result, it seemed possible that the United States might reach **zero population growth** (ZPG). ZPG is the state of population where the number of births plus immigrants equals the number of deaths plus emigrants. Sixty-five countries, most of them in Europe, are now at or approaching ZPG. According to the latest Census Bureau projections, however, the United States is not moving toward ZPG. Overall, U.S. fertility is on the rise because of the fertility rates among African Americans, Hispanics, and Asian Americans. Second, immigration rates are expected to remain high. Finally, despite the impact of the AIDS crisis, the nation's mortality rate is expected to decline while life expectancy will increase from the current figure of 77 years to 79 years by 2010. (374)

Functionalist Approach to Health and Illness: The **sick role** refers to societal expectations about the attitudes and behavior of a person viewed as being ill. Sociologist Talcott Parsons, well known for his contributions to functionalist theory, has outlined the behavior required of people considered "sick." According to Parsons, physicians function as "gatekeepers" for the sick role, either verifying a patient's condition as "illness" or designating the patient as "recovered." (376)

Conflict Approach to Health and Illness: Conflict theorists use the term **medicalization of society** to refer to the growing role of medicine as a major institution of social control. Medicine serves as an agent of social control by retaining absolute jurisdiction over many health care procedures. Viewed from a conflict perspective, there are glaring inequities in health care delivery within the United States. For example, poor and rural areas tend to be underserved because medical services concentrate where people are numerous and/or wealthy. Similarly, from a global perspective, there are obvious inequities in health care delivery. (376)

Interactionist Approach to Health and Illness: In examining health, illness, and medicine as a social institution, interactionists generally focus on microlevel study of the roles played by health care professionals and patients. They emphasize that the patient should not always be viewed as passive, but instead as an actor who often shows a powerful intent to see the physician. Sometimes patients play an active role in health care by *failing* to follow a physician's advice. (377)

Labeling Approach to Health and Illness: Labeling theorists suggest that the designation "healthy" or "ill" generally involves social definition by others. Just as police officers, judges, and other regulators of social control have the power to define certain people as criminals, health care professionals (especially physicians) have the power to define certain people as "sick." Moreover, like labels that suggest nonconformity or criminality, labels associated with illness commonly reshape how others treat us and how we see ourselves. Our society attaches serious consequences to labels that suggest less than perfect physical or mental health. (378)

Social Epidemiology and Health: **Social epidemiology** is the study of the distribution of disease, impairment, and general health status across a population. Studies in the United States and other countries have consistently shown that people in the lower classes have higher rates of mortality and disability. The poor economic and environmental conditions of groups, such as African Americans, Hispanics, and Native Americans are manifested in high morbidity and mortality rates for these groups. A large body of research indicates that, in comparison with men, women experience a higher prevalence of many illnesses. (380)

Pre-industrial, Industrial, and Postindustrial Cities: The **pre-industrial city**, as it is termed, generally had only a few thousand people living within its borders and was characterized by a relatively closed class system and limited mobility. The factory system that developed during the industrial revolution led to a much more refined division of labor than was evident in early pre-industrial cities. The many new occupations that were created produced a complex set of relationships among workers. Thus, the **industrial city** was not merely more populous than its pre-industrial predecessors, it was also based on very different principles of social organization. The **postindustrial city** is a city in which global finance and the electronic flow of information dominate the economy. (383)

Urbanization: The 1990 census was the first to demonstrate that more than half the population of the United States lived in urban areas of one million or more residents. During the nineteenth and early twentieth centuries, rapid urbanization occurred primarily in European and North American cities; however, since World War II, there has been an urban "explosion" in the world's developing countries. (385)

Functionalist View—Urban Ecology: **Human ecology** is concerned with the interrelationships between people and their spatial setting and physical environment. **Urban ecology** focuses on such relationships as they emerge in urban areas. Early urban ecologists, such as Robert Park and Ernest Burgess, concentrated on city life, but drew on the approaches used by ecologists in studying plant and animal communities. Urban ecologists trace their work back to the **concentric-zone theory** devised in the 1920s by Burgess. Families and business firms compete for the most valuable land; those possessing the most wealth and power are generally the winners. Because of its functionalist orientation, and its emphasis on stability, the concentric-zone theory tended to understate or ignore certain tensions apparent in metropolitan areas. As a response to the emergence of more than one focal point in some metropolitan areas, C.D. Harris and Edward Ullman presented the **multiple-nuclei theory**. In their view, a metropolitan area may have many centers of development, each of which reflects a particular urban need or activity. In a refinement of multiple-nuclei theory, contemporary urban ecologists have begun to study "edge cities," which have grown up on the outskirts of major metropolitan areas, and are economic and social centers with identities of their own. (385)

Conflict View—New Urban Sociology: Drawing on conflict theory, an approach that has come to be called the **new urban sociology** considers the interplay of local, national, and worldwide forces, and their effect on local space with special emphasis on the impact of global economic activity. The new urban sociology also draws on Immanuel Wallerstein's **world systems theory**. Wallerstein argues that certain industrialized nations (among them, the United States, Japan, and Germany) hold a dominant position at the **core** of the global economic system. They view cities not as independent and autonomous entities, but rather as the outcome of decision-making processes directed or influenced by a society's dominant classes, and by core industrialized nations. (388)

Central Cities: In 2000, some 226 million people, accounting for 80 percent of the nation's people, lived in metropolitan areas. Many urban residents are the descendants of European immigrants (Irish, Italians, Jews, Poles, and others) who came to the United States in the nineteenth and early twentieth centuries. In addition, a substantial number of low-income African Americans and Whites came to the cities from rural areas in the period following World War II. Even today, cities in the United States are the destinations of immigrants from around the world, including Mexico, Ireland, Cuba, Vietnam, and Haiti, as well as migrants from the U.S. commonwealth of Puerto Rico. (390)

Issues Facing Cities: Perhaps the single most dramatic reflection of the nation's urban ills has been the apparent "death" of entire neighborhoods. Such urban devastation has greatly contributed to the growing problem of homelessness. Another critical problem for the cities has been mass transportation. The federal government has traditionally given much more assistance to highway programs than to public transportation. Conflict theorists note that such a bias favors the relatively affluent (automobile owners), as well as corporations, such as auto manufacturers, tire makers, and oil companies. (391)

Suburban Expansion: Suburbanization has been the most dramatic population trend in the United States throughout the twentieth century. The suburban boom has been especially evident since World War II. From the perspective of new urban sociology, suburban expansion is far from a natural ecological process; rather, it reflects the distinct priorities of powerful economic and political interests. (392)

Diversity in the Suburbs: The common assumption that suburbia includes only prosperous Whites is far from correct. By 2000, for example, 34 percent of the Black population, 46 percent Latinos, and 53 percent Asians in the United States lived in the suburbs. Again in contrast to prevailing stereotypes, the suburbs include a significant number of low-income people from all backgrounds—White, Black, and Hispanic. Pollster Louis Harris has divided suburbs into four distinct categories: affluent bedroom communities, affluent settled communities, low-income growing communities, and low-income stagnant communities. (392)

Rural Communities: One-fourth of the population of the United States lives in towns of 2,500 people or less that are not adjacent to a city. In contrast to the historic stereotype of the farmer as a White male, African Americans and women have long played a significant role in agriculture in the United States. The postindustrial revolution has been far from kind to the rural communities of the United States. At the same time that farming has been in decline, so have mining and logging, the two nonagricultural staples of the rural economy. One consequence of rural decline is that policymakers have been confronted with an unpleasant task: deciding which ailing towns and counties will be supported with funds for economic development, and which rural communities will, in effect, be allowed to die. (393)

Social Policy—World Population Policy: Social policies that address population growth touch on the most sensitive aspects of people's lives: sexuality, childbearing, and family relationships. For this reason, reaching a global consensus on population issues has been difficult. In developing countries, the deathrate has fallen because of the introduction of modern medicine. In many developing countries, the traditional culture places great value on large families, thus the birthrate remains high. Parents also see children as potential laborers, and ultimately, as a means of broadening the family's economic base through the children's marriage. Yet functionalists note, when a country cannot provide clean water, food or shelter, high population growth *is* dysfunctional. Feminists question the motives of workers in government-funded population control projects who were distributing contraceptives without concern for health risks to meet government quotas. Conflict theorists have questioned why industrialized nations, such as the United States, are so concerned with controlling the population of developing countries. Conflict theorists note that population growth is not the cause of hunger and misery, but a result of unjust economic domination and exploitation of these countries. (395)

KEY TERMS

Briefly define or identify the following terms in the spaces provided below. The definitions of these terms can be found later in this chapter of the study guide.

Community	Demography
Fertility	Census
Vital statistics	Social epidemiology

Birthrate	Incidence
Total fertility rate	Prevalence
Deathrate	Morbidity
Infant mortality rate	Mortality rate
Life expectancy	*Curanderismo*
Growth rate	Pre-industrial city
Demographic transition	Industrial city
Population pyramid	Postindustrial city
ZPG	Urbanism
Health	Megalopolis
Sick role	Human ecology
Urban ecology	World systems analysis

Concentric zone theory	Defended neighborhood
Multiple-nuclei theory	Suburb
New urban sociology	

SELF-TEST

MODIFIED TRUE-FALSE QUESTIONS: If the statement below is true, write "true" in the space provided. If the statement is false, briefly correct the error.

1. Fertility is influenced by people's age of entry into sexual unions, and by their use of contraceptives, which reflect the social and religious values that guide a particular culture.

2. According to Thomas Robert Malthus, the gap between the food supply and world population will diminish over time.

3. The growth rate of a society is the difference between births and deaths.

4. Demographic transition in developing nations has involved a rapid increase in deathrates without adjustments in birthrates.

5. The sick role is an interactionist concept developed by Talcott Parsons, which refers to societal expectations about the attitudes and behavior of a person viewed as being ill.

6. Conflict theorists use the term *medicalization of society* to refer to the growing role of medicine as a major institution of social control.

7. Labeling theorists argue that labels associated with illness commonly reshape how others treat us and how we see ourselves.

8. Studies in the United States and in other countries have consistently shown that people in the lower classes have higher rates of mortality and disability than do more affluent people.

9. Researchers argue that women are much less likely than men to seek treatment, to be diagnosed as having diseases, and therefore to have their illnesses reflected in data examined by epidemiologists.

10. The industrial city is characterized by a relatively open class system in which social mobility is based significantly on ascribed characteristics.

11. The rise of suburban shopping malls is a vivid example of the phenomenon of multiple nuclei within metropolitan areas.

12. Edge cities are communities that have been built on the edge of waterways, mountains and other prominent geological features.

13. According to the world systems analysis, all nations prosper from a global economy.

14. The urban ecologists of the 1920s and 1930s were not ignorant of the role that the larger economy played in urbanization, but their theories emphasized the impact of local, rather than national or global forces.

15. Despite suburban diversification, race and ethnicity remain the most important factors distinguishing cities from suburbs in the United States.

MULTIPLE-CHOICE QUESTIONS: In each of the following, select the phrase that best completes the statement.

1. Karl Marx's work is important to the study of population because he linked overpopulation to
   a. migration.
   b. demographic transition.
   c. the sick role.
   d. the unequal distribution of resources.

2. Of the following nations, life expectancy at birth is highest in
   a. Japan.
   b. The United States.
   c. Gambia.
   d. all of the above

3. The final state in demographic transition is marked by
   a. high birthrates and death rates.
   b. high birthrates and low death rates.
   c. low birthrates and high death rates.
   d. low birthrates and low death rates.

4. The most recent period of high fertility in the United States, which began after the end of World War II, has often been referred to as the
   a. baby boom.
   b. baby bust.
   c. population bomb.
   d. age of Aquarius.

5. Demographers once believed the U.S. Population would stabilize between 290 and 300 million people. Now many believe that it will reach 404 million by 2050. This change in projections is due to
   a. the decline in the nation's mortality rate while life expectancy increases.
   b. rising fertility rates among African Americans, Hispanics, and Asian Americans.
   c. the fact that immigration rates are expected to remain high.
   d. all of the above

6. Which of the following is a criticism of the sick role?
   a. Patients' judgments regarding their own state of health may be related to their gender, age, social class, and ethnic group.
   b. The sick role may be more applicable to people experiencing short-term illnesses than those with recurring long-term illnesses.
   c. Even simple factors, such as whether a person is employed or not, seem to affect willingness to assume the sick role.
   d. All of the above.

7. Which sociological perspective would note that poor and rural sections of the United States tend to be underserved because medical services concentrate where people are numerous or wealthy?
   a. the functionalist perspective
   b. the conflict perspective
   c. the interactionist perspective
   d. the neo-Malthusian view

8. Which sociological perspective emphasizes that patients should not always be viewed as passive, but instead as actors who often show a powerful intent to see the physician?
   a. the functionalist perspective
   b. the conflict perspective
   c. the interactionist perspective
   d. labeling theory

9. In 1974, members of the American Psychiatric Association voted to drop ______________ from the standard manual of mental disorders.
   a. premenstrual syndrome
   b. homosexuality
   c. schizophrenia
   d. hyperactivity

10. Compared with Whites, Blacks have higher deathrates from
   a. heart disease.
   b. diabetes.
   c. cancer.
   d. all of the above

11. Urbanization in pre-industrial cities was restricted by
   a. reliance on animal power as a source of energy.
   b. the high levels of surplus produced by the agricultural sector.
   c. the ease of migration to the city.
   d. all of the above

12. Which group of sociologists notes that developers, bankers, and other powerful real estate interests view housing as an investment, and are primarily concerned with maximizing profit, not with solving social problems?
   a. urban ecologists
   b. new urban sociologists
   c. functionalists
   d. human ecologists

13. According to Herbert Gans, residents who remain in the city to take advantage of the unique cultural and intellectual benefits of the city are called
    a. cosmopolites.
    b. ethnic villagers.
    c. urban villagers.
    d. the trapped.

14. What proportion of employment in nonurban counties in the United States is accounted for by agriculture?
    a. 9 percent
    b. 22 percent
    c. 41 percent
    d. 63 percent

15. At the same time that farming has been in decline so have ____________ and ____________—the two nonagricultural staples of the rural economy.
    a. manufacturing; mining
    b. mining; logging
    c. extraction; manufacturing
    d. none of the above

FILL-IN QUESTIONS: Fill in the blank spaces in the sentences below with the correct words. Where two or more words are required, there will be a corresponding number of blank spaces.

1. In their studies of population issues, sociologists are keenly aware that various elements of population, such as ____________ and ____________ are profoundly affected by the norms, values, and social patterns of a society.

2. In the United States and most other countries, the ____________ is the primary mechanism for collecting population information.

3. ____________ ____________ ____________ is the average number of children born alive to any woman, assuming that she conforms to current fertility rates.

4. The growth rate of a society is the difference between births and deaths, plus the difference between ____________ and ____________.

5. Between 1700 and the mid-1900s there has been a gradual reduction in deathrates. People were able to live longer because of _____________ _____________ _____________ _____________, sanitation, _____________ and _____________ _____________ _____________.

6. From a _____________ perspective, "being sick" must be controlled so as to ensure that not too many people are released from their societal responsibilities at any one time.

7. _____________ theorists suggest that the designation of a person as "healthy" or "ill" generally involves social definition by others.

8. Contemporary social _____________ is concerned not only with epidemics but also with non-epidemic diseases, injuries, drug addiction and alcoholism, suicide, and mental illness.

9. Sociologists find it useful to consider _____________ rates because they reveal that a specific disease occurs more frequently among one segment of a population compared with another.

10. In the view of Karl Marx and contemporary _____________ theorists, capitalist societies such as the United States care more about maximizing profits than they do about the health and safety of industrial workers.

11. Louis Wirth distinguished three critical factors contributing to _____________: the size of the population, population density, and the heterogeneity of the population.

12. The urban ecology model is criticized by some for referring to the arrival of African Americans in white neighborhoods in the 1930s as an example of _____________ and _____________.

13. At the core of the city, according to the concentric zone theory, is the _____________ business district.

14. _____________ _____________ are communities that have grown up on the outskirts of major metropolitan areas, but are economic and social centers with identities of their own.

15. Gerald Suttles coined the term _____________ _____________ to refer to people's definitions of their community boundaries.

UNDERSTANDING SOCIAL POLICY: All of the following questions are based on material that appears in the social policy section on World Population Policy. Write a brief answer to each question in the space provided below.

1. Why has it been so difficult to reach a global consensus on population issues?

2. Functionalists would note that the best course of action for a community might differ from the best course of action for a society. What do they mean?

3. What is the Mexico City policy? Is it still in existence and how has it affected public health care programs?

DEFINITIONS OF KEY TERMS

Community: A spatial or territorial unit of social organization in which people have a sense of identity and a feeling of belonging. (368)

Fertility: The amount of reproduction among women of childbearing age. (368)

Demography: The scientific study of population. (369)

Census: An enumeration, or counting, of a population. (370)

Vital statistics: Records of births, deaths, marriages, and divorces gathered through a registration system maintained by governmental units. (370)

Birthrate: The number of live births per 1000 population in a given year. Also known as the crude birthrate. (370)

Total fertility rate (TFR): The average number of children born alive to a woman, assuming that she conforms to current fertility rates. (370)

Deathrate: The number of deaths per 1000 population in a given year. Also known as the crude deathrate. (370)

Infant mortality rate: The number of deaths of infants under one year of age per 1000 live births in a given year. (370)

Life expectancy: The average number of years a person can be expected to live under current mortality conditions. (371)

Growth rate: The difference between births and deaths, plus the difference between immigrants and emigrants, per 1000 population. (371)

Demographic transition: A term used to describe the change from high birthrates and deathrates to relatively low birthrates and deathrates. (371)

Population pyramid: A special type of bar chart that shows the distribution of population by gender and age. (373)

Zero population growth (ZPG): The state of a population with a growth rate of zero, achieved when the number of births plus immigrants is equal to the number of deaths plus emigrants. (374)

Health: As defined by the World Health Organization, a state of complete physical, mental, and social well-being, and not merely the absence of disease and infirmity. (375)

Sick role: Societal expectations about the attitudes and behavior of a person viewed as being ill. (376)

Social epidemiology: The study of the distribution of disease, impairment, and general health status across a population. (380)

Incidence: The number of new cases of a specific disorder occurring within a given population. (380)

Prevalence: The total number of cases of a specific disorder that exist at a given time. (380)

Morbidity rates: The incidence of diseases in a given population. (380)

Mortality rate: The incidence of death in a given population. (380)

Curanderismo: Latino folk medicine using holistic health care and healing. (381)

Pre-industrial city: A city with only a few thousand people living within its borders, which is characterized by a relatively closed class system and limited mobility. (383)

Industrial city: A city characterized by relatively large size, open competition, an open class system, and elaborate specialization in the manufacturing of goods. (384)

Postindustrial city: A city in which global finance and the electronic flow of information dominate the economy. (384)

Urbanism: A term used by Wirth to describe distinctive patterns of social behavior evident among city residents. (385)

Megalopolis: A densely populated area containing two or more cities and their surrounding suburbs. (385)

Human ecology: An area of study concerned with the interrelationships between people and their spatial and physical environment. (385)

Urban ecology: An area of study that focuses on the interrelationships between people and their environment in urban areas. (387)

Concentric-zone theory: A theory of urban growth devised by Ernest Burgess that sees growth in terms of a series of rings radiating from the central business district. (387)

Multiple-nuclei theory: A theory of urban growth developed by Harris and Ullman that views growth as emerging from many centers of development, each of which may reflect a particular urban need or activity. (387)

New urban sociology: An approach to urbanization that considers the interplay of local, national, and worldwide forces, and their effect on local space, with special emphasis on the impact of global economic activity. (388)

World systems theory: A view of the global economic system as divided between certain industrialized nations that control wealth, and developing countries that are controlled and exploited. (388)

Defended neighborhood: A neighborhood that residents identify through defined community borders, and through a perception that adjacent areas are geographically separate and socially different. (391)

Suburb: According to the Census Bureau, any territory within a metropolitan area that is not included in the central city. (391)

ANSWERS TO SELF-TEST

Modified True-False Questions

1. True (369)
2. According to Thomas Robert Malthus, the gap between the food supply and world population will increase over time. (369)
3. The growth rate of a society is the difference between births and deaths, plus the difference between immigrants and emigrants. (371)
4. Demographic transition in developing nations has involved a rapid decline in deathrates without adjustments in birthrates. (372)
5. The sick role is a functionalist concept developed by Talcott Parsons that refers to societal expectations about the attitudes and behavior of a person viewed as being ill. (376)
6. True (376)
7. True (378)
8. True (380)
9. Researchers argue that women are much more likely than men to seek treatment, to be diagnosed as having diseases, and therefore to have their illnesses reflected in data examined by epidemiologists. (382)
10. The industrial city is characterized by a relatively open class system in which mobility is based significantly on achieved characteristics. (384)
11. True (387)
12. Edge cities have grown up on the outskirts of major metropolitan areas and are economic and social centers with identities of their own. (388)
13. According to the world systems analysis, certain industrialized nations hold a dominant position at the *core* of the global economic system while poor developing nations are on the periphery of the global economy. (388)
14. True (389)
15. True (392)

Multiple-Choice Questions

1. d (369)
2. a (371)
3. d (372)
4. a (374)
5. d (375)
6. d (376)
7. b (377)
8. c (377)
9. b (379)
10. d (381)
11. a (383)
12. b (389)
13. a (390)
14. a (393)
15. b (393)

Fill-In Questions

1. fertility; mortality (369)
2. census (370)
3. Total fertility rate (370)
4. immigration; emigration (371)
5. advances in food production; nutrition; public health care (371)
6. functionalist (376)
7. Labeling (378)
8. epidemiology (380)
9. morbidity (380)
10. conflict (381)
11. urbanism (385)
12. invasion; succession (387)
13. central (387)

14. Edge cities (388)

15. defended neighborhood (391)

Understanding Social Policy: World Population Policy

1. Social policies that address population growth touch on the most sensitive aspects of people's lives: sexuality, childbearing, and family relationships. For this reason, reaching a global consensus on population issues has been difficult. (395)
2. In developing nations, parents see children as potential laborers, and ultimately as a means of broadening the family's economic base. Under such conditions, having fewer children may not appear to be a rational choice. Yet for a country that is struggling to provide clean water, food, and shelter to its people, high population growth is dysfunctional. (396)
3. In 1984, under President Ronald Regan, United States delegates to the World Population Conference in Mexico City announced that the United States would no longer support international planning programs that provided abortion services. During President Clinton's administration, this policy was overturned, but was reinstated when President Bush came into office. Currently, there is a gag rule imposed on all public health workers, which forbids them to discuss this option publicly or with their patients. This rule has polarized otherwise nonpartisan public health programs. (396)

CHAPTER 16

SOCIAL MOVEMENTS, SOCIAL CHANGE, AND TECHNOLOGY

KEY POINTS

Social Movements: Sociologists use the term **social movements** to refer to collective activities organized to bring about or resist fundamental change in an existing group or society. Social movements imply the existence of conflict, but we can also analyze their activities from a functionalist perspective, which views social movements as training grounds for leaders of the political establishment. (402)

Relative Deprivation: The term **relative deprivation** is defined as the conscious feeling of a negative discrepancy between legitimate expectations and present actualities. It may be characterized by scarcity rather than lack of necessities. A relatively deprived person is dissatisfied because he or she feels downtrodden relative to some appropriate reference group. A group will not mobilize into a social movement unless there is a shared perception that its relative deprivation can be ended only through collective action. (403)

Resource Mobilization: The term **resource mobilization** is used to refer to the ways in which a social movement utilizes such resources as money, political influence, access to the media, and personnel. Leadership is a central factor in the mobilization of the discontented into social movements. Karl Marx recognized the importance of recruitment when he called on workers to become aware of their oppressed status and to develop a class consciousness. (404)

New Social Movements: The term **new social movements** was introduced to refer to organized collective activities that promote autonomy and self-determination as well as improvements in the quality of life. Educated, middle-class people are significantly represented in some of these new social movements, such as the women's movement and the movement for lesbian and gay rights. (405)

Evolutionary Theory: **Evolutionary theory** views society as moving in a definite direction. Early evolutionary theorists generally agreed that society was inevitably progressing to a higher state. The writings of Auguste Comte and Émile Durkheim are examples of **unilinear evolutionary theory**. This approach contends that all societies pass through the same successive stages of evolution and inevitably reach the same end. **Multilinear evolutionary theory** holds that change can occur in several ways, and that it does not inevitably lead in the same direction. (405)

The Functionalist View of Change: Talcott Parsons, a leading proponent of functionalist theory, viewed society as naturally being in a state of equilibrium. According to his equilibrium model, as changes occur in one part of society, there must be adjustments in other parts. Parsons's approach explicitly incorporates the evolutionary notion of continuing progress. However, the dominant theme in this model is balance and stability. (407)

The Conflict View of Change: Conflict theorists contend that social institutions and practices continue because powerful groups have the ability to maintain the status quo. Change has crucial significance, since it is needed to correct social injustices and inequalities. In contrast to functionalists' emphasis on stability, Karl Marx argues that conflict is a normal and desirable aspect of social change. In fact, change must be encouraged as a means of eliminating social inequality. (408)

Resistance to Social Change: Efforts to promote social change are likely to meet with resistance. Social economist Thorstein Veblen coined the term **vested interests** to refer to those people or groups who will suffer in the event of social change. In general, those with a disproportionate share of society's wealth, status, and power have a vested interest in preserving the status quo. (409)

Computer Technology: **Telecommuters** are employees of business firms or government agencies who work full- or part-time at home rather than in an outside office. They are linked to their supervisors and colleagues through computer terminals, phone lines, and fax machines. The dramatic increase in use of the **Internet** (the world's largest computer network) has unquestionably contributed to the rise in telecommuting. Much of the focus of the Internet has been on new forms of communication and social interaction. Early users established a subculture with specific norms and values. Many troubling issues have been raised about day-to-day "life" on the Internet. In addition to issues concerning privacy and censorship, it has been noted that information is not evenly distributed throughout the population. The same people, by and large, who experience poor health and have few job opportunities have also been left off the information highway. (411)

Biotechnology: In the United States, the prenatal test of amniocentesis has been used for 20 years to ascertain the presence of certain defects that require medical procedures prior to birth. However, such tests inevitably identify the sex of the fetus, an outcome that has profound social implications. From a functionalist perspective, we can view sex selection as an adaptation of the basic family function of regulating reproduction. However, conflict theorists emphasize that sex selection may intensify the male dominance of our society and undermine the advances women have made in entering careers formerly restricted to men. One of the latest developments in genetic engineering is gene therapy. Such advances raise staggering possibilities for altering animal and human life forms, although gene therapy remains highly experimental. Because biotechnology has generally been seen as a benefit to society, critics have been concerned mostly with the possibility of unintended negative consequences, such as **bioterrorism**. (412)

Technological Accidents: Sociologist Charles Perrow introduced the term **normal accidents** to refer to failures that are inevitable given the manner in which human and technological systems are organized. In studying normal accidents, engineers focus on the system design, the physical environment, and the possibility of mechanical failure; social scientists evaluate possible human error. Given the serious consequences of a systems failure, we can anticipate that social scientists will work even more closely with engineers to explore how better equipment, training, and organization can reduce the likelihood of normal accidents. (414)

Social Control: With Big Brother watching and listening in more and more places, computer and video technology has facilitated supervision, control, and even domination by employers or government. There is a danger that electronic monitoring of employees can become a substitute for effective management and can lead to perceptions of unfairness and intrusiveness. Additionally, technological advances have created the possibility for a new type of white-collar crime: computer crime. It is now possible to gain access to a computer's inventory without leaving home, and to carry out embezzlement or electronic fraud without leaving a trace. (418)

Stratification and Inequality: An important continuing theme in sociology is stratification among people. Thus far, there is little evidence to suggest that technology will reduce inequality; indeed, it may only intensify it. A national study released in 2001 estimates that only 14 percent of the households earning less than $15,000 use the Internet, compared to 79 percent of those with incomes of $75,000 or more. Moreover, 56 percent of Asian American households and 46 percent of White households use the Internet, compared with 24 percent of Hispanic households and African American households. (419)

Privacy and Censorship in a Global Village: The whole issue of privacy and censorship in this technological age is another case of culture lag, in which the material culture (the technology) is changing faster than the nonmaterial culture (norms controlling the technology). Part of the problem is that computer technology has made it increasingly easy for any individual, business firm, or government agency to retrieve more and more information about any of us. Functionalists point to the manifest function of the Internet in its ability to facilitate communications. They also identify the latent function of providing a forum for groups with few resources to communicate with literally tens of millions of people. Conflict theorists note that there is the ever-present danger that a society's most powerful groups will use technological advances to invade the privacy of the less powerful, and thereby maintain or intensify various forms of inequality and injustice. Interactionists view the privacy and censorship debate as one that parallels concerns people have in other social interactions. Just as we may disapprove of some associations that relatives or friends have with other people, we also express concern over controversial Web sites and attempts to monitor people's social interaction. (419)

KEY TERMS

Briefly define or identify the following terms in the spaces provided below. The definitions of these terms can be found later in this chapter of the study guide.

Social movements	Multilinear evolutionary theory
Relative deprivation	Equilibrium model
Resource mobilization	Vested interests
False consciousness	Culture lag
New social movements	Luddites
Social change	Technology
Evolutionary theory	Telecommuters
Unilinear evolutionary theory	Normal accidents

SELF-TEST

MODIFIED TRUE-FALSE QUESTIONS: If the statement below is true, write "true" in the space provided. If the statement is false, briefly correct the error.

1. According to the relative deprivation approach, a disadvantaged group must perceive that it cannot attain its goals through conventional means.

2. Marginalized people are not involved in new social movements.

3. Whereas traditional views of social movements tended to emphasize resource mobilization on a broad global level, new social movements theory offers a local perspective on social and political activism.

4. Early evolutionary theorists generally agreed that society was inevitably progressing to a higher state.

5. In Roberta Garner's examination of virtual social movements, she indicates that like conventional social movements these virtual sites are generally not geared for action.

6. As noted by critics, the functionalist approach places substantial emphasis on the use of coercion by the powerful to maintain the illusion of a stable, well-integrated society.

7. The Marxist view of social change restricts people to a passive role in responding to inevitable cycles or changes in material culture.

8. Those with a disproportionate share of society's wealth, status, and power generally have a vested interest in preserving the status quo.

9. Nonmaterial culture encompasses ideas, norms, communication, and social organization.

10. In England beginning in 1811, masked craft workers known as Luddites conducted nighttime raids on factories and actually destroyed some of the new machinery.

11. Telecommuting is especially beneficial for one subordinate group: people with disabilities.

12. Between 1975 and August 2000, terrorists created 342 incidents involving biological or chemical agents.

13. Generally, 20 to 30 percent of normal accidents are attributed to human factors.

14. The emergence of cyberspace can be viewed as one step away from Ferdinand Tonnies's concept of *Gesellschaft* to the comparatively impersonal *Gemeinschaft*.

15. From a functionalist perspective there is the ever-present danger that a society's most powerful groups will use technological advances to invade the privacy of the less powerful, and thereby maintain or intensify various forms of inequality and injustice.

MULTIPLE-CHOICE QUESTIONS: In each of the following, select the phrase that best completes the statement.

1. Karl Marx held that a social movement would help workers overcome feelings of
   a. class consciousness
   b. false consciousness
   c. socialist consciousness
   d. surplus value

2. Nineteenth-century theories of social change reflect the pioneering work in biological evolution done by
   a. Albert Einstein.
   b. Charles Darwin.
   c. Harriet Martineau.
   d. Benjamin Franklin.

3. The writings of Auguste Comte and Émile Durkheim are examples of
   a. cyclical theory.
   b. unilinear theory.
   c. multilinear theory.
   d. conflict theory.

4. Which term was used by Talcott Parsons in asserting that society tends toward a state of stability or balance?
   a. charisma
   b. magnetism
   c. equilibrium
   d. status quo

5. ______________ ______________ theory holds that change can occur in several ways, and that it does not inevitably lead in the same direction.
   a. Unilinear evolution
   b. Value generalization
   c. Multilinear evolution
   d. Adaptive upgrading

6. The acceptance of preventative medicine is an example of the process that Parsons called
   a. differentiation.
   b. value generalization.
   c. Inclusion.
   d. adaptive upgrading.

7. Which sociological perspective minimizes change?
   a. the functionalist perspective
   b. the conflict perspective
   c. the interactionist perspective
   d. all of the above

8. Which of the following theorists argued that conflict is a normal and desirable aspect of social change?
   a. Karl Marx
   b. Talcott Parsons
   c. Émile Durkheim
   d. each of the above

9. The term *vested interests* was coined by social economist
   a. William F. Ogburn.
   b. Talcott Parsons.
   c. Auguste Comte.
   d. Thorstein Veblen.

10. The abbreviation "NIMBY" stands for "not in my backyard," a cry often heard when people protest
    a. landfills.
    b. prisons.
    c. nuclear power facilities.
    d. all of the above

11. Which sociologist introduced the concept of culture lag?
    a. William F. Ogburn
    b. Talcott Parsons
    c. Auguste Comte
    d. Thorstein Veblen

12. An example of global inequality is evident in Immanual Wallerstein's world system analysis, which states that
    a. core nations have a virtual monopoly on information technology.
    b. developing nations like Africa, Asia, and Latin America are on the periphery.
    c. periphery nations must rely on industrial giants for technology, and the information it provides.
    d. all of the above

13. Which term was introduced by Charles Perrow to refer to failures that are inevitable, given the manner in which human and technological systems are organized?
    a. the Perrow principle
    b. the Peter principle
    c. the school principal
    d. normal accidents

14. Internationally, which language dominates the Internet?
    a. English
    b. Russian
    c. German
    d. Japanese

15. Which sociological perspective would be especially interested in studying how people communicate with each other and develop relationships through MUDS (multi-user domains) and electronic chat rooms?
    a. the functionalist perspective
    b. the conflict perspective
    c. the interactionist perspective
    d. labeling theory

FILL-IN QUESTIONS: Fill in the blank spaces in the sentences below with the correct words. Where two or more words are required, there will be a corresponding number of blank spaces.

1. A relatively deprived person is dissatisfied because he or she feels deprived relative to some appropriate _______________ group.

2. CMC stands for _______________-_______________ _______________.

3. Early evolutionary theorists concluded in a (an) _______________ fashion that their own behavior and culture were more advanced than those of earlier civilizations.

4. _______________ evolutionary theory holds that change can occur in several ways, and that it does not inevitably lead in the same direction.

5. Talcott Parsons used the term _______________ to refer to the increasing complexity of social organization.

6. _______________ argued that conflict is a normal and desirable aspect of social change.

7. Social economist _______________ _______________ coined the term vested interests to refer to those people or groups who will suffer in the event of social change, and who have a stake in maintaining the status quo.

8. William Ogburn introduced the concept of culture lag to refer to the period of maladjustment during which the _______________ culture is still adapting to new _______________ conditions.

9. The term _______________ refers to those who are wary of technological innovations, and who question the incessant expansion of industrialization, the increasing destruction of the natural and agrarian world, and the "throw it away" mentality of contemporary capitalism.

10. _______________ is information about how to use the material resources of the environment to satisfy human needs and desires.

11. The _______________ is the world's largest computer network.

12. North America and Europe, and a few other industrialized nations, have the most _____________ _____________.

13. _____________ theorists contend that as we travel further and further along the electronic frontier, through advances such as telecommuting and the Internet, the disenfranchised poor may be isolated from mainstream society in an "information ghetto."

14. "Today we stand at the brink of becoming two societies, one largely white and plugged in and the other black and unplugged." This is how Black historian Henry Lewis Gates, Jr., starkly describes today's "_____________ _____________."

15. _____________ note that just as we may disapprove of some associations that relatives or friends have with other people, we also express concern over controversial Web sites, and attempt to monitor people's social exchanges.

UNDERSTANDING SOCIAL POLICY: All the following questions are based on material that appears in the social policy section on Privacy and Censorship in a Global Village. Write a brief answer to each question in the space provided below.

1. What is the functionalist view of privacy and censorship in a global village?

2. What is the conflict view of privacy and censorship in a global village?

3. What is the interactionist view of privacy and censorship in a global village?

4. Cite some of the global actions that have been taken to censor use of new technologies.

DEFINITIONS OF KEY TERMS

Social movements: Organized collective activities to bring about or resist fundamental change in existing society. (402)

Relative deprivation: The conscious feeling of a negative discrepancy between legitimate expectations and present actualities. (403)

Resource mobilization: The ways in which a social movement utilizes such resources as money, political influence, access to the media, and personnel. (404)

False consciousness: A term used by Karl Marx to describe an attitude held by members of a class that does not accurately reflect its objective position. (404)

New social movements: Organized collective activities that promote autonomy and self-determination as well as improvements in the quality of life. (405)

Social change: Significant alteration over time in behavior patterns and culture, including norms and values. (405)

Evolutionary theory: A theory of social change that holds that society is moving in a definite direction. (405)

Unilinear evolutionary theory: A theory of social change that holds that all societies pass through the same successive stages of evolution and inevitably reach the same end. (406)

Multilinear evolutionary theory: A theory of social change that holds that change can occur in several ways, and does not inevitably lead in the same direction. (406)

Equilibrium model: A functionalist view of society as tending toward a state of stability or balance. (407)

Vested interests: Those people or groups who will suffer in the event of social change and who have a stake in maintaining the status quo. (409)

Culture lag: A period of maladjustment when the nonmaterial culture is still adapting to new material conditions. (410)

Luddites: Rebellious craft workers in nineteenth-century England who destroyed new factory machinery as part of their resistance to the industrial revolution. (410)

Technology: Information about how to use the material resources of the environment to satisfy human needs and desires. (411)

Telecommuters: Employees of business firms or government agencies who work full- or part-time at home rather than in an outside office and who are linked to their supervisors and colleagues through computer terminals, phone lines, and fax machines. (412)

Normal accidents: Failures, which are inevitable given the manner in which human and technological systems are organized. (414)

ANSWERS TO SELF-TEST

Modified True-False Questions

1. True (404)
2. Marginalized people, among them homeless people, are involved in new social movements. (405)
3. Whereas traditional views of social movements tended to emphasize resource mobilization on a local level, new social movements theory offers a broad global perspective on social and political activism. (405)
4. True (405)
5. True (407)
6. As noted by critics, the functionalist approach virtually disregards the use of coercion by the powerful to maintain the illusion of a stable, well-integrated society. (408)
7. The Marxist view of social change does not restrict people to a passive role in responding to inevitable cycles or changes in material culture. (408)
8. True (409)
9. True (410)
10. True (410)
11. True (412)
12. True (414)
13. Generally, 60 to 80 percent of normal accidents are attributed to human factors. (415)
14. The emergence of cyberspace can be viewed as one step away from Ferdinand Tonnies's concept of the familiar, intimate *Gemeinschaft* to the comparatively impersonal *Gesellschaft*. (417)
15. From a conflict perspective there is the ever-present danger that a society's most powerful groups will use technological advances to invade the privacy of the less powerful, and thereby maintain or intensify various forms of inequality and injustice. (420)

Multiple-Choice Questions

1. b (404)
2. b (405)
3. b (406)
4. c (407)
5. c (406)
6. b (408)
7. a (408)
8. a (408)
9. d (409)
10. d (410)
11. a (410)
12. d (412)
13. d (414)
14. a (416)
15. c (416)

Fill-In Questions

1. reference (403)
2. computer-mediated communication (406)
3. ethnocentric (405)
4. Multilinear (406)
5. differentiation (407)
6. Marx (408)
7. Thorstein Veblen (409)
8. nonmaterial; material (410)
9. neo-Luddites (411)
10. Technology (411)
11. Internet (412)
12. Internet hosts
13. Conflict (419)
14. digital divide (419)
15. Interactionists (421)

Understanding Social Policy: Privacy and Censorship in a Global Village

1. Functionalists can point to the manifest function of the Internet in its ability to facilitate communications. They can also identify the latent function of providing a forum for groups with little resources to communicate with literally tens of millions of people. Thus, the functionalist perspective would see many aspects of technology fostering communication; the issue of censorship depends on how one views the content of the message, and the issue of privacy hinges on how information is used. (420)
2. Viewed from a conflict perspective there is the ever-present danger that a society's most powerful groups will use technological advances to invade the privacy of the less powerful, and thereby maintain or intensify various forms of inequality and injustice. Conflict theorists argue that control of technology in almost any form remains in the hands of those who already wield the most power, usually at the expense of the powerless and poor. (420)
3. Interactionists view the privacy and censorship debate as one that parallels concerns people have in any social interaction. Just as we may disapprove of some associations that relatives or friends have with other people, we also express concern over controversial Web sites and attempt to monitor people's social interaction. (420)
4. In Myanmar (Burma) the government has ruled that fax machines and computer modems are illegal. In Saudi Arabia, access to the Internet was banned until 1999. Now all Internet connections are routed through a government hub where computers block access to thousands of sites cataloged on a rapidly expanding censorship list, such as all gambling sites, all free-wheeling chat rooms, and all sites critical of the ruling Saudi family. By contrast, the openness of the Internet in other parts of the Middle East allows scattered Palestinian refugees to communicate with one another, and to establish Web sites that provide a history of Palestinian settlements. While China encourages expansion on the Internet, it has been very wary of facilitating communication that it regards as disruptive. Currently, the British government is constructing an Internet spy center to watch all online activity. (421)

NOTES

NOTES

NOTES

NOTES